MONEY SMARTS

THE GUIDE TO

INVESTING FOR

CURRENT INCOME

HOW TO B•U•I•L•D YOUR WEALTH
BY MASTERING THE BASIC STRATEGIES

THE GUIDE TO
INVESTING FOR
CURRENT INCOME

HOW TO B•U•I•L•D YOUR WEALTH
BY MASTERING THE BASIC STRATEGIES

by David L. Scott

The Globe Pequot Press

OLD SAYBROOK, CONNECTICUT

Library of Congress Cataloging-in-Publication Data

Scott, David Logan, 1942–
   The guide to investing for current income : how to build your wealth by mastering the basic strategies / by David L. Scott. — 1st ed.
     p.   cm.   — (Money smarts)
   Includes index.
   ISBN 1-56440-636-9
   1. Investments—United States. 2. Securities—United States. 3. Rate of return. 4. Finance, Personal. I. Title. II. Series: Scott, David Logan, 1942– Money smarts.
HG4910.S3917   1995
332.6—dc20   95-5889
                                          CIP

Manufactured in the United States of America
First Edition/First Printing

Contents

Acknowledgments

I express thanks to my graduate assistant and former student, Stefanie Webb, who read the manuscript and suggested numerous constructive changes. (I would like to be able to blame Stefanie for any remaining errors, but I'm afraid they are all mine.) I would also like to thank guitar-strumming Mace Lewis, my editor for the Money Smarts series and the resident troubadour of the Globe Pequot Press.

Introduction

Your local bank has reduced the interest rates it is paying on its various deposit accounts and you are wondering whether to reinvest the funds from a maturing certificate of deposit in another certificate with a lower interest rate or to withdraw the funds and seek another investment. If you transfer the funds, should you invest in stocks, buy bonds, choose an annuity product your insurance agent has been talking up, or buy a high-yielding mortgage pass-through security? Maybe you should consider one of the certificates of deposit touted by your broker. If you think bonds are the better choice, should you invest in a security with a maturity of eight to ten years or should you seek the higher current yield that is available on bonds with maturities of twenty-five years? It is important that you keep your current investment income as high as possible, but you don't want to put your money at risk. What should you do? Ah, I'm glad you asked. Read on!

Investing for current income has its advantages, especially if you need extra money to meet current living expenses. Even if you don't *really* need the income, it's comforting to know you will be receiving a certain amount of monthly or quarterly investment income. As a conservative investor, you may also sleep better at night owning investments with stable values, a characteristic enjoyed by many current-income investments. On the other hand, you should understand that owning current income investments has potential disadvantages, including modest yields, high taxes, and a small likelihood for major gains in value. And even though most current-income investments provide security of principal, the degree of security is subject to wide variations. Current income has its rewards, but at a cost.

If you have decided that current income is an important investment goal, you should understand the characteristics, risks, and potential returns available from various investments that provide this income. All investments that are desirable for the current income they produce are not created equal. Some investments are subject to fluctuations in market value, while other investments offer price stability but modest yields. The best investment for someone else may not be the best investment for you. You can intelligently choose a current income investment only if you are aware of the alternatives and you understand the fundamental investment characteristics of the alternatives.

The Guide to Investing for Current Income presents the risks and relative yields you can expect from investing in income-producing assets such as common stocks, preferred stocks, U.S. Treasury securities, corporate bonds, annuities, mortgage pass-through securities, and certificates of deposit. It compares these investments and provides guidance on how to go about building a portfolio that provides a relatively large amount of current income.

CHAPTER 1

Considerations When Investing for Current Income

A variety of investments are desirable for the current income they yield. Investments that produce large amounts of current income generally have limited growth prospects. Most types of current income are taxable in the year the income is received—a major disadvantage for investors in high tax brackets. Investments that produce current income have generally stable values but are subject to other types of risks. Assets that yield large amounts of current income are mostly of interest to conservative investors and individuals who need the income to meet current living expenses.

Investment assets typically yield one or both of two types of income: increases in value and current cash payments. Some investments, such as precious metals, undeveloped real estate, and stamp collections, produce no current cash payments but have the potential to yield substantial gains from increases in value. Other investments, such as savings accounts and certificates of deposit, produce current income but offer no potential for gains in value. Still other investments, such as preferred stocks, long-term corporate bonds, and certain common stocks, make current-income payments and are also subject to relatively large changes in market value.

Much can be said for owning investments that produce uniform monthly, semiannual, or annual cash payments. You are able to count on regular cash income that can be spent or, if the money isn't needed right away, reinvested to earn even larger amounts of income in future periods. Knowing that you will be receiving checks for a predetermined amount at regular intervals from social security, your pension fund, your employer, or an investment can produce a secure feeling and take some of the uncertainty out of your personal finances. A dependable stream of income pro-

---

Financial institutions that offer certificates of deposit are required by federal law to provide savers with the annual percentage yield (APY), which computes your return based on the annual rate, compounding frequency, and a 365-day year. Many methods are used to calculate yield and this standardized measure allows you to compare the yields being offered by different institutions.

vides a major boost to personal financial planning by allowing you to rely on a specific amount of income each planning period. Being able to count on a steady income allows you to spend current income or dip into savings with reasonable assurance that additional funds of a known amount will be forthcoming on a particular date to help with future house payments, grocery purchases, electric bills, college tuition, and other expenses.

Current investment income is not a universal investment goal. Individuals who already receive substantial amounts of current income may prefer to invest in assets that provide little current income but offer good potential for increases in value. Investing for growth not only offers the potential to earn higher returns, it also provides an opportunity for tax savings. Investments in collectibles, common stocks, and real estate—assets that can produce substantial gains (and losses) in value—often generate little or no current income that is subject to taxation. The remainder of this chapter is devoted to the comparative advantages and disadvantages of investing for current income.

Why Choose Investments That Produce Current Income?

Investments that yield substantial current income are not for everyone, but many investors prefer the financial security of receiving regular income that can be spent or reinvested. While some people thrive on taking major risks in an attempt to gain wealth, a large number of investors are just as happy going to bed knowing how much their assets will be worth the following morning.

Meet Current Spending Needs

Current income makes money available for food, clothing, shelter, entertainment, and other current expenses. Current income allows you to purchase goods and services without borrowing and to pay off previous borrowing. If there is no immediate need for the income, you can deposit the funds in your checking or savings account so that money will be available to pay upcoming bills or meet unexpected expenses.

Current income from investments is especially welcome when your earned income (salary or wages) is relatively modest and you have difficulty meeting essential spending needs. If you generally spend all or most of each paycheck, and the unpaid balances on your credit card accounts are steadily mounting, current income from investments can provide the extra funds that allow you to keep the credit cards securely in your purse or billfold and pay cash for the things you purchase.

Certainty of Return

Current income from an investment is generally more reliable than income you expect to derive from gains in an asset's value. Current income from an investment is usually stated both with respect to the amount of money you will receive and the dates the payments are to occur. On the other hand, estimates of an investment's expected price appreciation are often little more than guesses that frequently turn out to be wide of the mark. You may invest in common stocks, real estate, or collectibles with the anticipation of earning substantial returns from price appreciation, but these expected gains may not materialize or, if they do, may be much smaller than you anticipated. Most of the gains may occur after you become discouraged and sell the investment. In the real world, expected gains sometimes turn into actual losses.

Current investment income isn't always without risk, of course. The certainty of current income depends on the type of investment you own. Certificates of deposit and U.S. Treasury securities both provide a virtually ironclad guarantee that payments will be made as promised. Other investments, including common stocks and rental real estate, pay current income that is much more difficult to forecast accurately, especially five or ten years in the future. Companies sometimes encounter operating difficulties that cause them to eliminate or reduce substantially the dividends paid to stockholders. Likewise, vacancies can reduce cash income from a rental property to less than the mortgage payment. Various risks encountered by owners of current-income investments are discussed later in this chapter.

Stability of Value

Investments that provide substantial current cash payments in the form of dividends, interest, or other cash earnings generally have relatively limited potential for changes in

Think twice (or, maybe three times) about an investment that promises an unusually high yield. Chances are you are being misled about the yield or there are substantial risks you may be overlooking. Yield and risk generally go hand in hand. High yield means high risk.

value, either upward or downward. Savings accounts and certificates of deposit have no potential for value changes. Other than the current interest payments you may decide to reinvest or additional deposits you make, a savings account that is opened with a $10,000 deposit will remain a $10,000 savings account one year later, ten years later, or a hundred years later. Likewise, a $5,000 certificate of deposit remains a $5,000 certificate of deposit until the certificate matures and your principal is returned. The certificate increases in value only if you choose to have interest income reinvested rather than paid directly to you.

Even marketable investments such as bonds, preferred stocks, and common stocks that pay significant amounts of current income exhibit relatively modest changes in value compared to other investments that pay modest or no current income. Common stocks that pay large dividends (often called *income stocks*) typically underperform the stock averages in a rising stock market and outperform (that is, decline less than) other stocks during a falling stock market. In other words, income stocks ordinarily aren't subject to major price changes. Likewise, corporate and government notes and bonds exhibit a greater stability of value than common stocks do.

Stability of value is a desirable attribute for some investors, but not for everyone. Stable investments are un-

Don't choose tax-exempt investments for a tax-sheltered retirement account. Tax-exempt investments nearly always offer relatively low yields and the retirement account already shelters the income from taxation until withdrawal.

likely to lose much in market value, but they are also unlikely to produce significant gains. Investments with stable values appeal primarily to conservative investors and to individuals who may have to liquidate all or a portion of an investment on short notice.

Comparative Returns from Current-Income Investments

Expected returns (also called *yields*) from current-income investments generally differ from the returns investors expect to earn from investments that primarily offer gains in value. Expected returns are also different among the various types of current-income investments. Investments that pay current income differ with respect to risk, maturity, and taxability. Each of these factors can have a substantial impact on the return you can expect to earn from an investment.

Current-Income Investments compared to Investments Offering Increased Value

Because price appreciation tends to be considerably more uncertain than current income, investors will not normally commit their funds to investments that offer mostly gains in value unless the expected returns on those investments are relatively high. Most investment professionals and researchers believe that, over the long haul, investors *should expect to* earn higher returns by choosing assets with investment characteristics that cause the assets to change in market value. Undeveloped real estate should produce higher returns than common stocks, common stocks should pro-

Figure 1

THE IMPORTANCE OF COMPOUNDING

Compounding is computing interest earned on previously earned interest. Interest at the end of the first compounding period is calculated on the original principal, interest at the end of the second compounding period is calculated on the original principal *plus* interest earned in the first period, and so forth. The more frequently interest or dividend income is compounded, the higher the effective return you earn. The concept of compounding applies to various investments, including money market funds, Treasury bonds, corporate notes, and preferred stock. The compounding periods appropriate to a particular investment are a function of the number of times per year income is received or credited to your account. Interest on bonds involves semiannual compounding, dividends on stock involve quarterly compounding, and interest from certificates of deposit often involve daily compounding. The accompanying table illustrates the effect of various compounding methods at a nominal rate of 8 percent for a $1,000 deposit.

Frequency of Compounding

End of Year	Daily	Monthly	Quarterly	Semiannual	Annual
0	$1,000.00	$1,000.00	$1,000.00	$1,000.00	$1,000.00
1	1,083.28	1,083.00	1,082.43	1,081.60	1,080.00
2	1,174.39	1,172.89	1,171.66	1,169.86	1,166.40
3	1,271.22	1,270.24	1,268.24	1,265.32	1,259.71
4	1,377.08	1,375.67	1,372.78	1,368.57	1,360.49
5	1,491.76	1,489.85	1,485.95	1,480.25	1,469.33

duce higher returns than corporate bonds, and corporate bonds should produce higher returns than money market accounts. The higher returns cannot be expected every month, or even every year, but over many years of ownership, assets with capital gains potential should prevail.

The lower expected return from current-income investments stems from the relationship between risk and return. In general, risky investments offer higher expected returns compared to investments with less risk. Potential gains in value are usually more uncertain than current income, so investments that offer mostly price appreciation and little or no current income can be expected to produce higher returns over an extended period. Most finance experts advise young investors to assume the risk and construct an investment portfolio comprised largely of growth stocks that over time can be expected to produce larger returns than bonds and other current-income investments.

Comparative Returns among Current-Income Investments

Investments that pay current income do not all provide the same annual income or reward investors with identical yields. As mentioned, current-income investments differ with respect to risk, maturity, and taxability—factors that influence how investors view these income-producing assets. At the same time that tax-free money market funds yielded less than 2 percent during early 1994, some long-term corporate bonds, if held to maturity, promised an annual return of over 10 percent. The difference in return was influenced by all three of the factors just mentioned.

Assets that produce current income also vary with respect to the amount of money that must be invested. Corporate bonds issued in units of $1,000 each provide more annual current income than preferred stocks, which are often issued for $50 and $100 per share. The more money you invest in income-producing assets, the more current income you are likely to earn. *Current income* measures how much you receive, while *current return,* or *yield,* measures how much you receive in relation to the amount you invest or the amount the investment is worth.

Risk The return on an investment, including investments desired for current income, generally is directly related to the risk entailed in owning it. Yields on U.S. government bonds are always lower than yields on corporate bonds of the same maturity because corporate bonds are judged more risky with respect to whether all interest and principal ultimately will be paid. Likewise, yields on high-grade corporate bonds are lower than yields on low-grade corporate bonds. The higher the probability that promised income will not be paid, the higher the return that investors demand before they commit their money. Figure 2 illustrates the relationship between yield and risk for bonds of varying credit risk (including the possibility that interest and principal will not be paid in a timely manner).

Maturity Length Yields on current-income investments are generally higher the longer you are required to wait before the principal of the investment is returned. Certificates

---

Liquidity is important but can be overdone. Don't maintain unusually large balances in money market funds, savings accounts, and money market deposit accounts that generally provide relatively low yields. Too much liquidity means too little income.

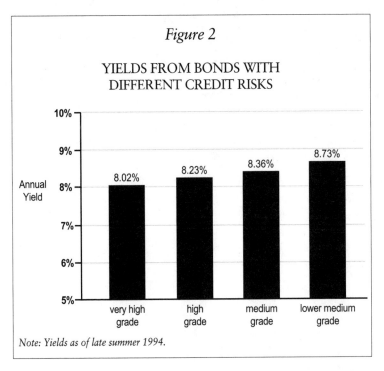

Figure 2

**YIELDS FROM BONDS WITH
DIFFERENT CREDIT RISKS**

Note: Yields as of late summer 1994.

of deposit (CDs) with ten-year maturities yield more than CDs with five-year maturities, which, in turn, yield more than one-year CDs. The same direct relationship between yield and maturity length also holds true for U.S. government, municipal, foreign, and corporate bonds. Bonds with long maturities of twenty and twenty-five years typically provide a higher yield than bonds with maturities of a few years. The relationship between annual yield and maturity length for U.S. Treasury securities in late 1994 is illustrated in Figure 3 with what economists call a *yield curve*. The upward slope of the yield curve is normal and indicates that Treasury yields were higher on securities with longer maturities.

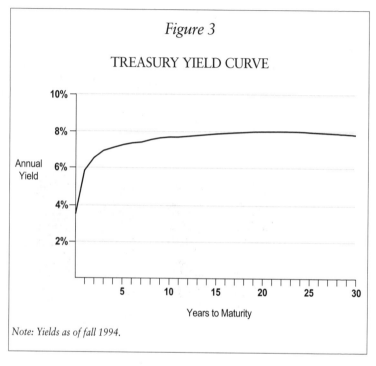

Figure 3

TREASURY YIELD CURVE

Note: Yields as of fall 1994.

Taxability Like most investors, you probably don't like to pay taxes and would accept a lower yield from an investment that allows you to earn nontaxable income. In fact, investments that pay tax-exempt income are available and they nearly always provide lower current returns *on a before-tax basis*. These investments may produce a larger after-tax return because no tax needs to be paid from the investment income that is received. In other words, the return you are promised is the return you keep.

Several types of investments pay current income that receives favorable tax treatment. Most bonds issued by states, cities, and political subdivisions pay interest that is not tax-

Figure 4

THE ADVANTAGE OF TAX-FREE INCOME
(Taxable Return Required to Earn Equivalent Yield)

Federal Tax Bracket	Tax-exempt Yield				
	2%	3%	4%	5%	6%
28.0	2.78%	4.17%	5.56%	6.94%	8.33%
31.0	2.90	4.35	5.80	7.25	8.70
36.0	3.13	4.69	6.25	7.81	9.38
39.6	3.31	4.97	6.62	8.28	9.93

able by the federal government and may be exempt from state and local taxes as well. U.S. Treasury securities pay interest that is exempt from state and local taxation, but not from federal taxation. Federal-agency securities pay interest income that *may* be exempt from state and local taxes, depending on the issuer, but are not exempt from federal taxation. Investments that receive favorable tax treatment are in such great demand, investors will accept a relatively low return compared to the return that could be earned on taxable investments. Institutions that are permitted to issue these securities enjoy a low cost of borrowing.

In summary, investments that provide large amounts of current income generally entail less risk and produce lower total returns compared to investments with the potential to produce large gains in value. All current income investments are not alike, and returns from owning these assets can vary depending on risk, maturity, and taxability.

The Tax Penalty of Current Income

An important disadvantage to owning investments that pay large amounts of current income is the relatively high tax rates applied to most of this income. Most forms of current investment income are taxed in the same manner as earned income, including wages and royalties. Current investment income is added to whatever other income you earn (most likely, your salary or wages) and taxed at the appropriate rate. The federal government and most states have a progressive tax system that stipulates higher tax rates on higher levels of taxable income. In other words, the larger your taxable income, including current investment income, the higher the tax rate you are required to pay on the *top* portion of that income.

Calculating Taxes on Current Investment Income

Figure 5 illustrates the applicable federal tax rates for tax year 1994. The schedule includes five successively higher brackets, which range from a low of 15 percent to a maximum of 39.6 percent. The rates apply to taxable income—income that has been adjusted for deductions and exemptions. Only the portion of taxable income that falls into each bracket is taxed at that bracket's respective rate. Suppose you are single with wages and other income of

Most investments are not federally insured. Never assume that an investment has federal insurance, even if you buy it from a commercial bank or a savings and loan association. Always ask.

Figure 5

SCHEDULE FOR CALCULATING
FEDERAL INCOME TAXES, 1994

Single

Taxable Income	Tax
$ 0 to $ 22,750	15.0%
22,750 to 55,100	$ 3,412.50 + 28.0% over $ 22,750
55,100 to 115,000	12,470.50 + 31.0% over 55,100
115,000 to 250,000	31,039.50 + 36.0% over 115,000
over $250,000	79,639.50 + 39.6% over 250,000

Married Filing Jointly

Taxable Income	Tax
$ 0 to $ 38,000	15.0%
38,000 to 91,850	$ 5,700.00 + 28.0% over $ 38,000
91,850 to 140,000	20,778.00 + 31.0% over 91,850
140,000 to 250,000	35,704.50 + 36.0% over 140,000
over $250,000	75,304.50 + 39.6% over 250,000

$26,000. Deductions and a personal exemption reduce your taxable income to $21,000. According to the schedule for individuals filing single returns in Figure 5, your tax liability would be 15 percent of $21,000, or $3,150. Now assume you earned an additional $3,000 of dividends and interest, resulting in taxable income of $24,000. According to the schedule in Figure 5, $1,750 of the extra income is taxed at 15 percent (taxable income to a maximum of $22,750 is taxed at 15 percent) and the remaining $1,250 is taxed at 28 percent, resulting in a total tax liability of $3,762.50. A little less than half of the additional current investment income is taxed at the higher rate of 28 percent.

From a tax standpoint, current investment income is most desirable for individuals with a modest taxable income. If you and your spouse file jointly and have $28,000 of combined taxable income, current investment income will be taxed by the federal government at only 15 percent. Likewise, if you are single with a taxable income of $40,000, 28 percent of additional current investment income must be paid in federal income taxes. At the opposite extreme, individuals and families with substantial amounts of earned and unearned income can pay tax rates of up to 39.6 percent on current investment income. These taxpayers are able to retain only 60 percent of the current investment income they earn.

Most personal income, including income you earn from investments, is taxable in the year the income is received or realized. Current investment income from dividends on common and preferred stock and interest earned from savings accounts, certificates of deposit, and most bonds is taxable in the year you receive credit for it. Thus, you must pay taxes on interest earned from a certificate of deposit in

Investing in most current-income investments means that you are sacrificing any chance at large capital gains. On the other hand, current-income investments tend to provide you with some protection against major declines in the value of your principal.

the year the interest is paid, even if you have directed the financial institution to automatically reinvest the interest. Paying taxes currently on dividend and interest income may not seem objectionable, because most other income is taxed in the same manner; but it pales in comparison with the manner in which long-term capital gains are treated for tax purposes.

Capital Gains Taxation

Gains in the value of capital assets receive special tax treatment both with respect to when a tax must be paid and the tax rate that is applied. The special tax treatment accorded to most capital gains causes gains in the value of capital assets to be more valuable than an equal amount of current investment income.

The taxable gain on the sale of an investment equals the difference between the cost, or *basis,* of the asset and the proceeds received from the sale of the asset. Suppose you purchase 50 shares of Coca-Cola common stock at a price of $40 per share, and several years later sell the same shares at a price of $48 per share. The brokerage firm that executed the transactions charged $80 for making the purchase and $90 to sell the stock. For tax purposes your cost basis equals $40 times 50 shares, or $2,000, plus the $80 commission, or $2,080. Proceeds from the sale equal $48 times 50 shares, or $2,400, less the $90 commission you were charged, or $2,310. Taxable income from the sale equals $2,310 less $2,080, or $230. The same procedure is used to calculate the gain and taxable income when selling shares of a mutual fund. Special tax rules may apply to bonds and notes purchased at other than face value.

Cost Basis		Proceeds from Sale	
Stock purchase	$2,000	Stock sale	$2,400
plus: Commission	80	less: Commission	90
Cost basis	$2,080	Net proceeds	$2,310

$$\begin{array}{r} \$2,310 \\ -\ \underline{\$2,080} \\ \textit{Net Capital Gain}\ =\ \$230 \end{array}$$

Increases in the value of a capital asset generally are not subject to taxation until the asset is sold and the gain is realized. A paper profit (the increase in the market value of an investment you continue to own) generally is not taxable. Because only realized gains need be included in taxable income, taxes on an increase in an asset's value can be postponed so long as you don't sell the asset. Taxes can be delayed for years or decades, or even forever if you hold an appreciated asset until your death. Appreciated assets that become part of an estate are inherited with a cost basis equal to their respective values on the date of death.

A second tax advantage of realized gains in value compared to current investment income stems from the lower tax rate that *may* apply to the gains. Currently, realized gains on investments held over one year are taxed at a maximum rate of 28 percent. If your total taxable income is relatively small, a realized gain may be taxed at only 15 percent, the same rate applied to other taxable income. The lower tax rate is applicable if the addition of a capital gain to your other income does not cause taxable income to spill over into the 28 percent tax bracket. Otherwise, part of the gain is taxed at 15 percent and the remainder is taxed at an effective rate of 28 percent.

In summary, most types of current income suffer a double whammy from taxes; income becomes taxable as soon as it is received, and the applicable tax rate is likely to be relatively high if you have a large salary or substantial amounts of unearned income (which includes investment income).

The Risks of Investing for Current Income

Risk is the uncertainty of an outcome. The tenure of your employment, safe arrival at your destination, and your health are all subject to various risks. The risk of an investment is generally defined as the uncertainty of the return the asset will provide. The less certain you are regarding the return you will earn, including both current income and changes in value, the greater the risk of owning a particular asset. Actually, risk is somewhat more complicated than this because the riskiness of a particular asset affects the overall risk of your investment portfolio. Risky assets of one type can sometimes be combined with risky assets of another type and result in a risk that is less than for each of the individual assets taken alone. This concept of portfolio risk is very important, but a detailed discussion is best left to a more advanced book on investments.

Long-term bonds generally offer high yields but are subject to major price fluctuations. These investments also subject you to the risk that inflation will eat away at the purchasing power of your interest income. Thus, even bonds with the highest credit quality subject you to certain types of risks.

All investments entail some risk, although the degree of riskiness can vary substantially between different types of investments. As mentioned previously, investments purchased primarily for current income tend to have less variability of return and less total risk than investments desired for the potential capital gains they are expected to produce; but even current income investments have risks, some of which are sometimes overlooked. The remainder of this section discusses some important risks involved in owning investments that provide relatively large amounts of current income.

Business Risk of the Organization in Which You Invest

Business risk is defined by the uncertainty of revenues and of operating expenses for the organization in which you invest. Dividend payments on common or preferred stock are subject to being decreased or eliminated if the business experiences declining revenues or increasing costs. A dividend reduction or even the possibility of a reduction is likely to have a negative effect on a company's stock price. An airline may be hit with reduced revenues because of a price war or with higher fuel costs. Likewise, a company that mines copper ore may encounter a long strike or a weak market for its product. Both these occurrences could lead to a decision to reduce temporarily or eliminate dividends to stockholders.

The business risk applicable to a particular organization is influenced by numerous factors. Uncertain revenues that are subject to large fluctuations make it difficult for an investor to feel secure about anticipated dividend payments to the owners of a company's common stock. Likewise, fluctuating costs that are not accompanied by offsetting changes in revenues can cause a company to reduce or omit dividend payments. A large proportion of fixed costs can have a major impact on a firm's ability to meet its operating expenses. Automotive manufacturers that substitute robotics for human employees in an attempt to achieve increased efficiencies and product quality are unable to force the robots to take a hike if sales decline. The costs related to the robots continue regardless of what happens to sales. The bottom line is that organizations with uncertain revenues and costs place your investment income and the value of your investment at risk.

Financial Risk of the Organization in Which You Invest

Financial risk relates to the degree to which an organization uses borrowed money to pay for operations and the purchase of assets. The greater the degree to which an organization relies on borrowed money, the greater the uncertainty regarding payments the organization makes to its creditors, its stockholders, or both. Financial risk applies to some governmental organizations as well as to private ones.

Many investments purchased primarily for current income are subject to little or no financial risk. Securities issued by the U.S. Treasury are considered very secure, even though the government owes creditors *trillions* of dollars.

Money market funds offered by brokerage firms are not federally insured but are generally very safe. Compare yields available from these funds with yields offered by money market deposit accounts at depository institutions when deciding on where to park your short-term money.

After all, the U.S. Treasury prints currency! Certificates of deposit and savings accounts at federally insured depository institutions are free of credit risk, although the failure of a depository institution may cause a delay in your payments or a reduction in the interest rate your funds earn.

At the opposite extreme, debt issued and guaranteed only by the promise of a company that has become a financial basket case entails a great amount of financial risk. The finances of a company can deteriorate to such an extent that bondholders and other creditors may wonder if even the next interest payment will be forthcoming. Creditors of a debt-burdened city or county are likely to find that promised interest payments and return of principal are both at risk. The more a city relies on debt to finance its expenditures, the more likely the city will encounter difficulty in making interest and principal payments. Likewise, if you own the bonds or notes of a company that is heavily in debt, there is cause for concern regarding the interest and principal that are promised.

Price-Level Risk

Price-level risk (also called *inflation risk* and *purchasing power risk*) refers to uncertainty regarding the real value of the cash payments you expect to receive. You may be certain of receiving promised payments without knowing the value of those payments at the time they are received. Price-level risk results from unexpected increases in the prices of goods and services, usually measured by changes in the Consumer Price Index. Unexpected inflation causes a larger decrease in the purchasing power of payments compared to the decrease that was expected at the time the investment

Figure 6

EFFECT OF INFLATION ON THE PURCHASING
POWER OF A $1,000 FIXED PAYMENT

Year	Annual Inflation Rate					
	2%	4%	6%	8%	10%	12%
1	$980	$962	$943	$926	$909	$893
2	961	925	890	857	826	797
3	942	889	840	794	751	712
4	924	855	792	735	683	636
5	906	822	747	681	621	567
6	888	790	705	630	564	507
7	871	760	665	583	513	452
8	853	731	627	540	467	404
9	837	703	592	500	424	361
10	820	676	558	463	386	322
15	743	555	417	315	239	183
20	673	456	312	215	149	104
25	610	375	233	146	92	59
30	552	308	174	99	57	33

was made. An extended period of high inflation rates can result in interest and dividend income that buys few goods and services. Figure 6 illustrates the extent to which persistant inflation eats away at the purchasing power of a series of fixed payments.

Individuals who own current-income investments such as bonds with lengthy maturities and preferred stocks are particularly prone to price-level risk because a fixed number of dollars will be received over a long period. Short-term current-income investments subject investors to substantially less inflation risk because money that has been invested is returned and available for reinvestment before inflation can cause much damage. Unexpected inflation influences expected levels of future inflation and drives up interest rates. Rising interest rates allow the owner of a short-term investment to earn a higher return on reinvested funds.

Interest Rate Risk

Interest rate risk refers to the uncertainty of an investment's return because of changes in value caused by interest rate changes. Changes in market interest rates have a strong impact on the market value of long-term fixed-income investments such as bonds and preferred stocks. An increase in interest rates causes a decline in the market value of all types of fixed-income investments. Conversely, interest rate declines cause outstanding fixed-income investments to increase in price. The extent to which investment values are affected by interest rate changes is a function of the length of time over which the fixed payments are scheduled. A given change in interest rates has a greater impact on the price of a bond with a thirty-year maturity than on the price of a Treasury security with a one-year maturity.

Reinvestment Risk

Reinvestment risk is the uncertainty with respect to the return you will be able to earn on reinvested cash. The greater the amount of cash you will have available to reinvest and the more uncertain the return you will earn on these reinvestments the greater the reinvestment risk of owning a particular investment. If you expect to spend most or all of an investment's cash flow (dividends, interest payments, and principal, for example), reinvestment risk is nil because there will be no reinvestment. On the other hand, if you reinvest principal and rely on investment income to pay for most of your living expenses, or if you typically reinvest both principal and investment income, reinvestment risk is very important.

Investments that pay large amounts of current income generally subject investors to substantial amounts of reinvestment risk compared to investments that are purchased mostly for expected capital gains. A stock that pays a high dividend carries a greater amount of reinvestment risk than a stock without a dividend (one where, for example, all of a company's earnings are used to purchase additional assets). Likewise, short-term debt securities that require frequent reinvestment of principal entail substantially more reinvestment risk than long-term debt securities that mature many years in the future.

Liquidity Risk

Liquidity risk is uncertainty regarding the ease with which you will be able to convert an investment to cash. Some investments can be difficult to liquidate (sell) at a reasonable price for a variety of reasons. Many corporate and municipal bonds are infrequently traded and thus they can be hard to sell; as a result, you will probably receive less than mar-

> Your investment goals play a major role in determining the type of investment portfolio you should own. Establish your investment goals before you begin making investments.

ket value if you sell bonds before they mature. Likewise, depository institutions generally impose financial penalties on savers who liquidate a certificate of deposit prior to the scheduled maturity date. Real estate investments have liquidity risk, particularly during periods of high interest rates, when many potential buyers are unable to qualify for financing.

Some stocks and bonds are actively traded and can be easily sold at or near market value. Treasury securities trade in large volume and can be purchased or sold at current market prices. Likewise, hundreds of thousands of shares of some widely held stocks are regularly traded each day. Active trading produces good liquidity. Short-term investments scheduled to return your principal in a matter of weeks or several months allow freedom from worry about liquidity because it is unlikely the investments will have to be sold. And owning some short-term investments allows you also to purchase assets with longer maturities with less worry that you may have to liquidate them prematurely and suffer a loss. If a need for cash arises, you can liquidate the short-term investments.

Market Risk

Market risk is uncertainty of an investment's future value because of unpredictable market fluctuations. The market values of many investments are in a constant state of flux. Asset values constantly move up and down, making it difficult to determine the exact value at which assets will sell on any particular date in the future. Tangible assets, common stocks, low-quality bonds, and real estate are subject to substantial market risk. How much will your 1953 Mickey

Mantle baseball card bring in the event you need to sell it six months from today? At what price will Motorola common stock sell in three months? On the other hand, savings accounts, certificates of deposit, and short-term debt securities are subject to little or no market risk.

Market risk is important only if you may be required to liquidate an investment on relatively short notice. If sudden liquidation is unlikely, fluctuations in the value of an asset shouldn't be a concern. In any case, most investments purchased for current income are subject to a relatively small amount of market risk compared to investments desired for their capital gains potential. In fact, the lack of market risk of many types of current-income investments is a main attraction for investors who may need their funds in a hurry.

Should You Invest for Current Income?

The priority you place on current income as an investment goal should depend on several factors that were discussed earlier in this chapter. Investments that pay relatively large amounts of current income may be just what the financial doctor ordered if you need additional income to meet current spending needs. Likewise, a nominal income and a low rate of federal and state taxes make current income relatively desirable because you are able to retain most of the dividend and interest income you receive. Also, if you are a conservative investor who prefers investments with stable market values there are few alternatives to invest in assets that pay high current income. Investments that are desired for their capital gains potential tend to exhibit large fluctuations in market values.

CHAPTER 2

Short-Term Investments That Provide Current Income

Short-term investments are desirable primarily for their liquidity and security, and secondarily for the current income they provide. Investments with maturities of a year or less are subject to minor fluctuations in value, an important advantage if you are a conservative investor who may find it necessary to tap your savings. Most short-term investments are of relatively high credit quality, so there is little worry about interest not being paid or principal not being available. Short-term investments generally provide only a modest return, a price you must pay when you may need to raise cash on relatively short notice.

You are nearly certain to own at least some short-term investments. Passbook savings accounts, interest-bearing checking accounts, money market accounts, certificates of deposit, Treasury bills, and money market mutual funds are all part of the huge offering of short-term investments that capture the excess funds of individual investors. You may be ultraconservative financially and demand that all your investments be insured and instantly accessible. Perhaps you are investing to meet short-term goals that will soon require that you access a substantial portion of your savings.

Every individual and family should own some investments that can be liquidated on short notice without loss of value. You want access to funds in the event there is a need to repair your automobile, fix the roof on your home, or replace a refrigerator that conks out. You need to be able to count on having funds available that can be used to pay the deductible portion of potential insurance claims or to tide you over several months of unemployment in case you are unable to work or are laid off by your employer. There are many other unexpected spending needs you are likely to encounter that are best met with a reserve of liquid assets. It is to your advantage to maintain a pool of assets that can be accessed on short notice. While these assets won't provide much current income, you should invest to earn as high a return as possible.

Of course, you can always choose to leave your savings intact and borrow any funds that you require on short notice. Instead of withdrawing funds from your money market deposit account you can write a check against your home equity loan's line of credit. Choosing this option allows you to build a portfolio comprised mostly of long-term investments with reduced liquidity and higher expected returns; but relying on borrowing to meet immediate cash requirements may turn out to be a relatively expensive alternative because short-term loans often carry high fees and interest charges that result in a cost that exceeds the returns that are being earned on your investments. Why borrow at an annual interest cost of 12 percent when your investments are providing an average return of only 8 percent?

Characteristics of Short-Term Investments

Short-term investments generally offer excellent liquidity and security, but typically produce relatively meager returns, nearly all of which are in the form of current income. Certain short-term investments can be liquidated without penalty whenever you choose. Other short-term investments must be sold or surrendered at a penalty if you need the cash from your investment returned prior to maturity. Regardless, the maturities of most short-term investments are sufficiently limited that waiting several weeks or months for the return of your funds generally doesn't prove to be a major hardship.

The liquidity, safety, and yield characteristics of short-term investments make these assets an appropriate part of any individual's investment portfolio, although when used to excess they will generally penalize the portfolio's return. Still, combining a reasonable amount short-term assets with intermediate- and long-term investments allows adequate access to cash without requiring that you liquidate real estate, stock, or long-term bonds at an inappropriate time.

Liquidity

Short-term investments can normally be readily converted to cash and thus offer superior liquidity, which is the major advantage of owning these assets. Some short-term investments can be instantly converted to cash without expense or loss of value. Liquidating other short-term investments incorporates a small degree of uncertainty regarding the price you will receive, requires that you pay a fee, or both. In virtually all instances the fee is nominal. In any case, the maturities of short-term investments are so limited that you generally must wait only a short time until your principal is returned without your paying a fee or suffering a loss of value.

Safety of Principal

Most short-term investments offer substantial safety of principal. In other words, when investing in the majority of short-term assets you can be certain that all the money that has been promised will be returned and that you will receive the money on the scheduled date. Several short-term investments even include a U.S. government guarantee that your principal will be returned. The principal of some other short-term investments is guaranteed by a U.S. government agency. Guarantees by the U.S. government and its agencies

Avoid tax-exempt investments unless you are in at least the 28 percent federal income tax bracket. Tax-exempt investments are more beneficial the higher your income tax bracket. Be sure to consider state taxes as well as federal taxes when you select a tax-favored investment.

cause assets to be riskless from the standpoint that your principal will be returned. Other short-term investments are less secure and depend on the quality of the promise that is made by the organization in which you invest.

Certainty of Income

Certainty of income is the likelihood that income payments will occur as expected. The more sure you are of the income you will earn and the date the income will be paid, the greater the certainty of income. In general, short-term investments have great certainty of income in terms of actually receiving investment income on the anticipated date. Nevertheless, the characteristics of certain short-term investments make it difficult to determine exactly how much income will be earned. For example, it is not possible to know exactly how much income will be earned from an investment in a money market mutual fund or a money market account. On the other hand, a six-month certificate of deposit with a set interest rate offers total assurance of interest income that will be earned.

Reinvestment Risk

Reinvestment risk is a major problem common to all short-term investments. By definition, short-term investments return the principal relatively quickly, at which time you must either spend the money you receive or reinvest your funds at whatever return is available at the time you receive them. Suppose you are currently earning an annual return of 8 percent on a $40,000 six-month certificate of deposit. The certificate will produce $1,600 in interest income six months after your investment [.08 × $40,000 × (6 months/12 months)]. Suppose that when the certificate matures you must reinvest the principal at a time when 7 percent is the best available return. Your semiannual income will fall to $1,400 [.07 × $40,000 × (6 months/12 months)], a 12.5 percent decline from the $1,600 income you earned on the matured certificate. The reduction in income means you must now cut back on your spending if the interest income is needed for regular living expenses. A decline in current investment income proved to be the fate of many retirees in the 1980s and early 1990s, as short-term interest rates plunged from the high teens to the low single digits.

Stability of Value

All short-term investments have stable values. In fact, some types of short-term investments, including money market accounts and money market funds, have fixed prices. The market price of a U.S. Treasury bill can vary slightly but is quite stable compared to most other investments. The price stability of short-term investments is a great advantage for an investor who is not concerned about earning capital gains, but you must remember that price stability works in both directions. You don't have to worry about the value of your investment declining, but you also lack the opportunity for an increase in market value to boost your total yield above that provided by current income.

Yield

Short-term investments typically provide investors with relatively low yields. A comparatively small return is the price you pay for the safety, liquidity, and price stability that is offered by short-term assets. The relationship between maturity length and return was discussed in Chapter 1 and illustrated by the yield curve in Figure 2. Yields on short-term investments occasionally rise above the yields on intermediate- and long-term investments, but not often. Short-term interest rates exceeding long-term rates is unusual and temporary, and is nearly always occasioned by widespread expectations that interest rates will soon be falling.

Types of Short-Term Investments

Several types of short-term investments are available to provide you with liquidity and a modest return. Although all short-term assets tend to have similar characteristics as described above, there are some differences with regard to risk and return of which you should be aware. For example, some short-term investments are guaranteed by the U.S. government while other investments are not. Also, some short-term investments allow you to write checks to tap your funds, but other investments do not. Some short-term investments even pay income that is not subject to certain taxes. The type of short-term investment you choose matters, but not always a lot.

Remember that insured certificates of deposit are offered by brokerage firms as well as by banks, savings and loans, and credit unions. CDs distributed by brokerage firms sometimes offer higher yields than you can obtain locally. No brokerage commissions are charged to you on these brokered CDs.

NOW Accounts

A NOW account (in formal terms, a *negotiable order of withdrawal account*) is an interest-bearing checking account or, viewed somewhat differently, a savings account with check-writing privileges. You may not consider this type of account to be an investment, but a NOW account does pay current income at the same time it temporarily serves as a place to park funds you expect to spend or invest.

NOW accounts were introduced in the early 1970s and increased in popularity during the early 1980s when short-term interest rates soared to record levels. These accounts are a product of the financial deregulation that swept the nation in the 1970s and 1980s. No federal limits are imposed on the yield a financial institution is permitted to pay or the minimum account balance that must be maintained in order to earn interest income. Individual institutions are permitted to establish monthly fees and determine the minimum balances customers must maintain to earn interest income. Most institutions require that customers maintain a minimum balance of between $500 and $1,000 to earn interest, although some institutions have no minimum and pay interest on any account balance. The freedom of individual financial institutions to establish their own yields and

---

When you don't have much money to invest, a mutual fund is probably a better choice than individual stocks and bonds. Mutual funds offer professional management and diversification, two particular advantages if you invest relatively modest amounts of money. Also, brokerage commissions on small trades often consume too large a proportion of your capital.

minimum balance requirements means that it is worthwhile to shop among competing institutions for the best deal.

Yield NOW accounts generally pay minimal yields that are similar to the rates available on passbook savings accounts, although some institutions pay bonus yields on balances above a specified level. For example, your account may earn an annual yield of 3.0 percent on balances up to $2,500 and 3.25 percent on all balances above that level. Unfortunately, fees charged by some institutions can wipe out most earnings and cause your account to be at best a break-even investment on all but very high balances. Yields on NOW accounts are highest when short-term market rates of interest are high, but these accounts tend to provide one of the lowest yields available on any investment. On the other hand, the yield is always positive; that isn't true of the total yields earned on many other investments.

Risk NOW accounts at insured commercial banks, savings and loan associations, and credit unions subject your funds to minimal risk. The balance in your account up to $100,000 is insured by an agency of the U.S. government. This insurance means there is no risk that $100,000 of your investment will be lost in the event there is a failure of the financial institution holding your funds. Since your investment has a stable value, you are always able to get out what you put in. The account value is not influenced by market fluctuations or by changing interest rates and varies only because of withdrawals, deposits, and additions of interest to the principal. NOW accounts at the same time offer the ultimate in liquidity, because you are able to write a check at any time and withdraw any or all of your funds.

Summary: NOW Accounts NOW accounts allow you to earn a nominal return on funds you would normally park in a checking account. You should maintain a relatively small balance in one of these accounts unless you have recently deposited funds that are awaiting reinvestment or will be used to make a major purchase. Balances you maintain for an emergency fund or for some expected expenditure several months down the road are likely to earn a higher return with equally good liquidity in one of the other investments discussed in this chapter.

Money Market Deposit Accounts

Money market deposit accounts (MMDAs) were introduced in the early 1980s to provide commercial banks, savings and loan associations, and credit unions with a financial product that had a return competitive with the high yields then being offered by money market mutual funds (discussed below) sold by brokerage firms and mutual funds. The new product was an immediate success, partly because people felt comfortable having their funds invested in a familiar local institution, and partly because many of the institutions offered above-market interest rates to attract money away from competitors. Some institutions were so successful at attracting money into the money market deposit accounts that they placed limits on the amount of funds any one individual was permitted to deposit.

Money market deposit accounts don't provide investors with the same degree of flexibility as NOW accounts. For example, there is generally a limit of six checks or transfers (such as automatic payments from the account) per month. There is also likely to be a stipulated minimum amount for each check that is written. Greater activity typically results in a fee being charged by the institution holding the account, although you may get away with a warning the first time you exceed the stipulated number. The limit imposed on check writing and transfers is not an average. You are not permitted to write checks above the limit in one month because you wrote fewer than the permitted number in the preceding month. Most financial institutions require that a minimum balance (usually $1,000 or $1,500) be maintained in the account in order to have interest credited.

Yield Yields on money market deposit accounts are generally quite low, although they are somewhat higher than the returns available on NOW accounts. After paying federal and state income taxes on the interest income, you will be lucky to earn a return that equals the inflation rate. Thus, money you invest in money market accounts should just about maintain its purchasing power but won't fare much better.

Yields on money market deposit accounts generally follow the trend of yields on other short-term investments, although not at exactly the same pace. When short-term market rates of interest increase, yields on MMDAs also increase, but often at a slower pace, and when short-term market rates of interest decline, yields on money market deposit accounts tend to decline, but more slowly. Yields on money market deposit accounts are established by the individual institutions that offer them. As a result, the yields

Investment company expenses have an important effect on the yield you will earn from owning income funds. Before you invest money, carefully read an investment company's prospectus and examine the fees you will be required to pay.

may be higher or lower than the yields that are being offered on similar investments, depending on how badly a particular financial institution needs additional deposits. A bank or savings and loan association with heavy loan demand is likely to increase the yields offered on its savings instruments, including MMDAs, in order to attract additional deposits. On the other hand, during a period of weak loan demand, financial institutions will have little reason to increase yields offered to depositors so that yields on money market deposit accounts will lag behind yields on most other short-term investments.

Risk Risks associated with the funds you have invested in a money market deposit account are identical to the risks previously discussed for funds invested in NOW accounts. MMDAs at insured financial institutions have no credit risk because the principal of your investment is insured by an agency of the U.S. government. So long as your total deposits at the financial institution do not exceed the insurance limit you can be assured that your funds will be available in the event the institution fails. Although check writing and transfers are severely restricted compared to the same privileges on NOW accounts, which generally have no limits, your invested funds have substantial liquidity and can be withdrawn at any time. The principal of your investment has a stable value that changes only because of deposits, withdrawals, and the addition of interest income. The account value is not affected by interest rate movements or by changing investor expectations. In other words, there is no interest rate risk or market risk.

The major risk you face when funds are deposited in a money market deposit account is the possibility of declining interest income caused by falling yields. If the interest income from a money market deposit account supplies a major portion of your spendable income, there is a substantial risk: Short-term interest rates can experience a sharp decline, causing your financial institution to lower the rate it pays on money market deposit accounts. In the worst case, you may find that your annual income is reduced by 50 percent or more following a major decline in short-term interest rates. At the opposite extreme, if short-term interest rates experience a sharp increase, the yield you earn on your money market deposit account should also increase, although perhaps not at the same rate.

Summary: Money Market Deposit Accounts A money market deposit account is a low-risk and low-return investment that should primarily serve as a way station for funds that are awaiting reinvestment or a major expenditure. The liquidity and insurance cause your funds to be accessible and safe. A MMDA has such restricted checking privileges that it cannot substitute for a regular checking account. In this respect, an MMDA is not as useful as a NOW account which generally provides unlimited checking along with modest interest income on balances held in the account. On the upside, a money market deposit account usually provides a somewhat higher return than either a NOW account or a passbook savings account; however, on an after-tax basis you can expect little more than to keep up with inflation.

Money Market Funds

A money market fund is a specialized type of mutual fund that pools the money contributed by investors (who purchase ownership units, or *shares,* and become *shareholders* of the fund) and purchases short-term money market securities such as Treasury bills, commercial paper, certificates of deposit, and banker's acceptances (see Figure 7). Money market securities are typically sold in very large denominations that are beyond the financial means of all but the most wealthy individual investors. For example, commercial paper is denominated in amounts of $100,000 and above. The money market fund collects interest income from the investments it owns and passes this money along to its shareholders. The more income the money market fund earns from the securities it owns, the more income it has to pay to its shareholders. Money market funds that meet certain established standards, including the payment of virtually all investment income to shareholders, are not required to pay income taxes on their earnings. A more detailed discussion of mutual funds is in Chapter 5.

Money market funds were created in the 1970s when interest rates on money market securities were substantially higher than the returns that individuals could earn at commercial banks and savings and loan associations. The funds became an immediate hit and remained very popular even after financial deregulation permitted depository institutions to offer competitive products.

Money market fund managers stabilize the price of their funds' shares at $1. Unless a financial calamity causes substantial declines in the market values of securities owned by a fund, you can be confident that 5,000 shares of a money market fund you purchase for $5,000 can later be redeemed for $1 each, or $5,000. Shares of most funds can be redeemed for cash by writing checks (usually for a specified minimum) or by phoning or writing the distributor or sponsor of the fund. You can generally have proceeds from redeemed shares wired to another financial institution.

Figure 7

INVESTMENTS OF
MONEY MARKET MUTUAL FUNDS

Money market mutual funds invest in money market securities and pass along to shareholders the interest income the funds earn. Money market securities are actively traded and entail little credit risk. These securities are generally issued in very large denominations.

Banker's acceptances are drafts that an accepting bank promises to pay on a specific future date. Acceptances are traded at a discount from the specified amount to be paid (generally $100,000 and above). Credit risk is relatively small because payment is guaranteed both by a business and the accepting bank.

Certificates of deposit (CDs) are large deposits ($100,000 and over) placed in commercial banks at a stated rate of interest. Large CDs are negotiable and are regularly bought and sold in the secondary market. Except for the part covered by federal insurance, the credit quality of certificates of deposit is a function of the financial strength of the issuing bank.

Commercial paper is an unsecured short-term promissory note (270 days or less) issued by manufacturing firms and finance companies. These notes of $100,000 and over are traded in the secondary market. The credit quality of commercial paper is a function of the financial strength of the issuer.

Repurchase agreements (repos) are contractual agreements to buy and sell U.S. government securities at specified prices on specific dates. Interest on a repo is the difference between the price at which which a security is sold and the price at which the seller agrees to repurchase the security. The transaction is essentially a loan by the institution that purchases the security and agrees to resell the same security later.

U.S. Treasury bills are short-term obligations of the U.S. Treasury sold at a discount to face value. The bills mature at face value with interest income equal to the difference between the price paid and the amount received. Treasury bills are issued in $10,000 denominations and are very actively traded in the secondary market. Treasury bills have no credit risk.

Sponsors of some money market funds choose to sell their shares directly to investors while other funds sell shares through distributors such as brokerage firms and financial planners. Many brokerage companies sponsor their own money market funds.

Differences among Money Market Funds Unlike money market deposit accounts, which are essentially identical from one institution to the next (except for relatively small differences in yield), money market mutual funds can embody important differences. For example, fund sponsors set up varying requirements for opening an account. Some money market funds require as little as $500 to $1,000 for individuals to open an account, while other funds require a deposit of $2,500 or more. Requirements for subsequent purchases are generally substantially lower.

Funds also differ with respect to the types of money market securities that are purchased and held. Money market funds regularly alter the maturities of the securities they hold, a practice that affects the current yield and the yield you will earn in future weeks and months. (This topic is discussed more fully below, in the section on yield.) Funds also differ with respect to the type and quality of the securities they select. Some funds have an aggressive investment philosophy and are willing to hold securities with more risk in order to increase the income they earn. The managers of the more aggressive money market funds attempt to attract in-

---

Pay attention to the commissions charged by brokerage firms. Wide differences exist in the commissions charged by different firms. Choosing a low-cost brokerage firm can save you substantial amounts of money, especially if you are an active investor.

vestors' money by earning high income that will provide shareholders with relatively high yields. Other money market funds restrict their investments to very high-quality money market securities.

Tax-exempt Money Market Funds A large number of money market funds restrict the investments in their portfolios to federally tax-exempt securities issued by states, counties, cities, and other political subdivisions. Tax-exempt securities pay interest that is free from federal income taxes. Dividends paid to the shareholders of tax-exempt money market funds are also exempt from federal income taxes and sometimes from state and local taxes as well. Whether dividends you receive from a particular money market fund are exempt from state and local income taxes depends on the tax laws of the state in which you reside. Most, but not all, states exempt income earned from tax-exempt securities issued in those particular states. For example, the shareholder of a money market fund that invests in tax-exempt securities issued in Georgia is not required to pay federal or Georgia income taxes on dividends received from the fund. On the other hand, a Georgia shareholder is required to pay state and local taxes on interest income the fund earns from securities issued by cities and states outside Georgia. Many tax-exempt money market mutual funds restrict their portfolios to tax-exempt securities of a particular state in order to attract investment funds from residents of that state who want to avoid paying state and local taxes as well as federal taxes.

Fees Money market mutual funds are not organized or operated as charities, so expect to incur fees when you place money in one of these investments. Although generally no sales or redemption fees are charged, a fund's sponsor must cover the expenses incurred in managing and operating the

---

Figure 8

EXPENSES LISTED IN A TYPICAL MONEY MARKET FUND PROSPECTUS

Shareholder Transaction Expenses

Maximum Sales Charge Imposed on Purchases (as a percentage of purchase price)	None
Sales Charge Imposed on Dividend Reinvestment	None
Deferred Sales Charge (as a percentage of original purchase price or redemption proceeds, whichever is lower)	None
Exchange Fee	None

Annual Fund Operating Expenses (as a percentage of average net assets) for the year ended June 30, 1995

Investment Advisory Fees	0.48%
12b-1 Fees	0.25%
Other Expenses	
Custodial Fees	0.01%
Shareholder Servicing Costs	0.08%
Other	0.01%
Total Other Expenses	0.10%
Total Fund Operating Expenses	0.83%

fund—postage, electric bills, pencils, paper, property taxes, and so forth. Portfolio managers who select the securities to buy and sell must be paid. Likewise, the firm must pay employees to handle correspondence and maintain the fund's records. Most fund sponsors maintain toll-free telephone service for investors. Some have automated systems that allow you to determine current yields on the funds.

Operating and management expenses that are incurred by a money market fund are taken care of with a periodic fee that is charged against the fund's income. Thus, a portion of the interest income earned by money market funds is consumed by expenses before dividends are paid to shareholders. Some funds also charge a separate annual fee that is used to pay for marketing expenses. This charge, called a *12b-1 fee,* directly reduces the yield you earn from a money market fund. The 12b-1 fee is tacked on top of the operating and management expenses that all money market funds charge. All fees and other charges are spelled out in each fund's *prospectus,* a free booklet you should obtain from the distributor before investing any of your money in any mutual fund.

Expenses can eat away a significant portion of a money market fund's income, especially when short-term interest rates are relatively low. Expenses of a fund remain relatively constant regardless of how much income a fund earns from its investments. Thus, these expenses consume a larger portion of income when short-term interest rates and fund income are low. On the other hand, fixed expenses appear less important when short-term interest rates are high and a fund earns substantial amounts of interest income.

Yield Yields on money market funds closely track short-term interest rates on Treasury bills and certificates of deposit, two investments that comprise a major portion of these funds' portfolios. Yields on money market funds increase during periods when short-term interest rates are increasing, and decrease when short-term rates decline. Yields on money market funds tend to change more slowly than Treasury bill rates, depending on the maturity lengths of securities that are being held by a particular fund. The longer the maturity of the securities that are owned the more the change in the yield on a fund will lag behind changes in interest rates on money market securities such as Treasury bills. A relatively long average maturity of the securities owned by a money market fund is desirable when short-term interest rates are falling because the yield on the fund will not decline as rapidly as market rates. Likewise, a short average maturity of a money market fund's portfolio is desirable when short-term interest rates are rising.

The yield provided by a particular money market fund depends both on the maturity lengths and the credit quality of the securities the fund owns. Portfolio managers of money market funds can increase stockholder yields by investing in securities with greater credit risk that have higher yields. For example, a fund manager might purchase certificates of deposit from a bank or savings and loan of questionable financial strength because the interest rate on the certificates issued by that institution is higher than the inter-

---

Don't put your money into investments you don't understand. Complicated investments often involve high fees and high risk. You are likely to encounter fees and risks you didn't know existed.

est rates that are available on CDs from stronger financial institutions.

Risk Money market funds generally provide substantial safety. The majority of investments owned by these funds are of high credit quality, so there is little possibility you will suffer a loss of principal. Moreover, the shares have a stable market value, so you know exactly how much money you will receive when all or part of your investment is liquidated. Changing interest rates do not affect the market value of your shares, although they do affect the yield you earn from owning the shares. It is generally inadvisable to invest a large amount of money in a money market account because of the relatively low yield and substantial uncertainty concerning the income you will earn. Short-term interest rates on money market securities that are owned by money market funds are subject to sudden movements that can cause dividend income to undergo equally sudden changes.

Summary: Money Market Mutual Funds A money market fund is a special type of mutual fund that offers price stability, safety, and superb liquidity. These desirable characteristics are at least partially offset by relatively low yields. A money market fund is a good place to park money you may need in a hurry and funds you intend to reinvest. Yields on money market funds, like other short-term investments, are subject to abrupt and unexpected fluctuations that can result in rapid changes in investment income. The low return makes it unwise to maintain large balances in money market funds for long periods of time. You can often earn substantially higher returns by choosing investments with maturities of two or three years.

Certificates of Deposit

Certificates of deposit (CDs) are available with maturities that range from three months to several years. These investments thus qualify as short-term or intermediate-term depending on the maturity that is chosen. Yields on short-term CDs are affected by yields on other short-term investments and also by financial institutions' need for funds. During periods when banks and savings and loan associations are flush with cash and have only a modest loan demand, yields on certificates of deposit tend to be below the yields available on Treasury bills of equal maturity. During periods of heavy loan demand, CD yields are likely to be more competitive. Yields on short-term certificates of deposit generally change more slowly than Treasury bill yields.

Certificates of deposit are discussed more fully in the next chapter, which focuses on intermediate-term investments. Other than variations in yield caused by maturity differences, intermediate-term and short-term certificates of deposit are identical.

U.S. Treasury Bills

U.S. Treasury bills (also called *T-bills*) are short-term debt obligations of the federal government that are auctioned at a discount and redeemed at face value. Bills with maturities of 13 weeks and 26 weeks are auctioned by the U.S. Trea-

Don't acquire an investment until you first determine whether any fees or penalties will be assessed to liquidate it. This caution applies to all investments including certificates of deposit, annuities, and mutual funds.

sury each Monday and bills with a maturity of fifty-two weeks are auctioned each month. These negotiable securities are frequently bought and sold many times before maturity. Because the secondary market in U.S. Treasury bills is very active, these securities have great liquidity. Treasury bills are issued in minimum denominations of $10,000.

No direct interest is paid to owners of Treasury bills. Interest income to an investor is the difference between the price paid and the price received when a bill is sold or redeemed. A $10,000 Treasury bill purchased for $9,800 and held to maturity will produce $200 of interest income. The lower the price you pay for a T-bill, the more interest income you will earn. Treasury bills always sell at a discount from face value; otherwise, a buyer would suffer a loss (that is, earn negative interest). Prices are quoted as a percentage of face value. For example, a quote of 98.933 indicates a price of $9,893.30

Treasury bills may be purchased directly from the Federal Reserve (which conducts the auctions for the U.S. Treasury) or bought through a commercial bank or brokerage firm, both of which charge a nominal fee. Most individuals who purchase Treasury bills directly from the Federal Reserve do so with a noncompetitive tender that can be obtained from any Federal Reserve bank. The tender allows you to purchase one or more bills without being required to bid a specific price. You pay a price equal to the weighted average price of the bonds sold to competitive bidders. You are not required to submit a tender if a bank or brokerage firm purchases bills for your account. Brokerage firms and banks are able to purchase Treasury bills that trade in the secondary market. This allows you to acquire bills with maturities of other than 13, 26, and 52 weeks. For example,

Figure 9

TREASURY BILL AUCTION RESULTS, MAY 31, 1994

	13-week bills	26-week bills
Applications	$58,287,417,000	$48,440,911,000
Accepted bids	$12,793,031,000	$12,706,690,000
Accepted at low price	34%	24%
Accepted noncompetitively	$ 1,341,207,000	$ 1,095,274,000
Average price (rate)	98.931 (4.23%)	97.639 (4.67%)
High price (rate)	98.933 (4.23%)	97.644 (4.66%)
Low price (rate)	98.931 (4.23%)	97.634 (4.68%)
Coupon equivalent	4.33%	4.85%

Note: Issues were dated June 2; 13-week bills matured on Sept. 1, 1994; 26-week bills matured on Dec. 1, 1994. Coupon equivalent equates rate on Treasury bills to quoted rate on coupon securities.

you can purchase a bill with an original maturity of 26 weeks that was issued 22 weeks earlier and has 4 weeks remaining to maturity. Thus, you need wait only 4 weeks to have the bill redeemed at its $10,000 face value.

Treasury bills fluctuate in market value, but not much. The market price of a bill trading in the secondary market is influenced by short-term interest rates. An increase in short-term interest rates will cause an outstanding Treasury bill to decline in value (the bill must provide a higher yield to attract buyers), while a decline in short-term interest rates will cause an increase in the market price of a T-bill trading in the secondary market. Price fluctuations are minor because of the short time investors must wait before a bill is redeemed at face value. For example, a Treasury bill scheduled to mature in three weeks will not sell at much below face value even when short-term interest rates experience a substantial increase. Thus, at the time you purchase a T-bill, it is not possible to determine the exact price you will receive if you must sell the security before maturity; however, you can expect to receive a price that is between the price you paid and the value at maturity.

Yield Treasury bill yields track short-term interest rates, so the returns from owning these investments are relatively low. Yields are generally similar to yields on money market funds (which frequently own lots of Treasury bills) and short-term certificates of deposit. Treasury bill yields tend to change more rapidly than the yields on either of these other investments. When short-term interest rates are declining, T-bill yields will tend to decline more rapidly than yields on CDs, money market funds, and money market deposit accounts. Likewise, Treasury bill yields increase more rapidly than these other investments when short-term interest rates are rising.

If you decide to acquire individual bonds, choose maturity lengths that will allow you to hold them to redemption. Bonds you sell prior to the scheduled redemption dates are likely to involve a price penalty, and you will always be required to pay a brokerage commission. Redemptions at face value occur without any expense to you.

One major advantage of owning Treasury bills is the exemption of interest income from state and local taxation. Of course, the exemption is important only if you are a resident of a city or state that levies a personal income tax. Investors who reside in high-tax states such as New York and California realize substantial financial benefit from the tax exemption. At the same time, investors residing in Nevada, Florida, and other states without a personal income tax receive no tax benefit from owning these securities. (Some states do levy a relatively small intangible tax on the market value of securities.)

The quoted yield on a Treasury bill is applicable to the period from the date of purchase to redemption. In other words, if you hold a bill to maturity you will receive the quoted yield over the holding period. This is different from money market accounts and money market mutual funds, which produce varying yields. Of course, when a T-bill matures and you decide to reinvest the proceeds in another bill, you will have to accept whatever yield is available at that time. In this respect, a Treasury bill is identical to a certificate of deposit.

Calculating the Yield on a Treasury Bill An earlier section mentioned that income from owning a Treasury bill is the difference between the cost at which a bill is purchased and the proceeds received when the bill is sold or redeemed. No periodic interest payments are made to owners of Treasury bills. T-bills are generally quoted on the basis of the discount from face value. A *bid discount* is the discount a dealer will demand to purchase a bill and the *ask discount* is the discount a dealer will accept to sell a bill. Remember, a larger discount means a lower price. Thus, the bid discount is always higher (that is, the price is lower) than the ask discount.

Figure 10

TREASURY BILL QUOTATIONS, MAY 26, 1994

Maturity	Days to Mat.	Bid	Ask	Change	Ask Yld.
Jun 02 '94	2	3.98	3.88	+0.21	3.91
Jun 09 '94	9	3.77	3.67	+0.06	3.72
Jun 16 '94	16	3.84	3.74	+0.19	3.80
Jun 23 '94	23	3.73	3.63	+0.06	3.69
Jun 30 '94	30	3.72	3.68	+0.05	3.74
Jul 07 '94	37	3.73	3.69	+0.01	3.76

Figure 10 illustrates the conventional form in which Treasury bill quotations are published. The left column denotes the date on which each issue will mature and the second column indicates the number of days until these bills reach maturity. The bid discount and the ask discount listed in the center columns indicate that dealers are offering to purchase the June 30 bill at a discount of 3.72 percent and sell the same bills with a discount of 3.68 percent. The higher discount on the dealers' offer to purchase bills represents a price that is lower than the price at which the dealers will sell bills.

Quoted discounts are annualized to make the discounts comparable among bills with different maturities. Thus, calculating the price of a bill requires that the discount be adjusted to account for the length of time a bill will remain outstanding. Suppose you wish to calculate the prices at which you can purchase and sell Treasury bills with thirty days remaining to maturity.

$$\text{Dealer's Ask Price} = \text{Par} - (\text{Discount})(\text{Days to Maturity}/360)$$
$$= 100 - (3.68)(30/360)$$
$$= 100 - .3067$$
$$= 99.693$$

$$\text{Dealer's Bid Price} = 100 - (3.72)(30/360)$$
$$= 100 - .3100$$
$$= 99.690$$

By convention, Treasury bill prices are quoted as a percentage of face value. In this instance the price you must pay to purchase the bond (using the dealer ask price) is 99.693 percent of $10,000.00, or $9,969.30. Using the dealer bid price, you would receive 99.690 percent of $10,000.00, or $9,969.00 if you sell the bill. Be aware that listed quotations are generally for very large trades and you are likely to pay a higher price and receive a lower price than indicated by the posted quotations.

The annualized effective simple yield (indicated by *Ask Yld.* in the last column of Figure 10) for a Treasury bill is calculated as follows:

$$\frac{365 \times \text{Quoted Annual Discount Rate}}{360 - (\text{Annual Discount Rate} \times \text{Days to Maturity})}$$

$$= \frac{365 \times .0368}{360 - (.0368 \times 30)}$$

$$= .0374, \text{ or } 3.74\%$$

Thus, purchasing the thirty-day bill at the indicated price would provide you with a simple annualized yield of 3.74

percent. This yield does not take into account the effect of compounding, the earning of interest on interest. The simple yield just calculated is slightly less than the compound yield that assumes that all the proceeds including interest income are reinvested throughout the year.

Be aware that financial reports concerning yields for both weekly Treasury bill auctions and Treasury bill yields in the secondary market generally utilize the annualized discount, not the annualized effective yield, and that this causes yields on Treasury bills to be understated relative to the yields reported on other types of securities.

Summary: Treasury Bills   Treasury bills can prove to be an excellent short-term investment. These securities often provide a higher yield than other short-term investments, especially on an after-tax basis, because interest income earned from Treasury bills is not subject to state and local taxation. Treasury bills are easy to purchase (although a small commission will be charged if you go through a brokerage firm or commercial bank) and are equally easy to sell in the event you decide to sell bills before maturity. You are able to determine the exact amount of income you will earn if you hold a bill to maturity and there is no possibility of default. One major disadvantage for many investors is the large minimum denomination ($10,000) in which Treasury bills are issued.

Shop for the highest yield on a certificate of deposit. Financial institutions in the same town pay different interest rates. This can make a major difference in your interest income, especially if you choose CDs with maturities of five years and more.

CHAPTER 3

Intermediate-Term Investments That Provide Current Income

Intermediate-term investments that are desirable for their current income—U.S. Treasury notes, corporate notes, and CDs—are a compromise between the relatively low yields and excellent liquidity of short-term investments and the higher yields and higher market risk of long-term investments. Intermediate-term investments are an appropriate choice for conservative investors who desire yields higher than are available on money market funds and money market deposit accounts and who are willing to accept some but not a lot of fluctuations in the principal value of their investments. For investors seeking current income, intermediate-term investments can be combined with short-term and long-term investments to provide a balanced portfolio.

Intermediate-length investments that produce current income are a compromise choice. They generally offer somewhat lower yields than are available on long-term investments but higher yields than can be earned from owning short-term investments. Current-income investments with intermediate-length maturities of two to ten years offer greater liquidity than many long-term investments but less liquidity than short-term investments. If you are yearning for a higher return than you are currently being paid by the local bank on your money market deposit account but you are reluctant to commit your savings for twenty-five or thirty years, an intermediate-term investment may be just what you are seeking, so long as you understand that you will not enjoy the instant liquidity offered by most short-term investments. You can get your money out of an intermediate-term investment prior to the scheduled maturity, but you may incur a fee, a partial loss of principal, or both. On the positive side, intermediate-term investments can sometimes be liquidated at a profit.

Although nearly all intermediate-term investments that pay relatively high levels of current income enjoy the same general investment characteristics, these investments are certainly not identical. Some have the backing of government insurance and some do not. Some can be sold before maturity to another investor in the secondary market, while others cannot. Some pay income that is sheltered from certain

Don't buy an investment when you are being pressured for a quick decision. Investment decisions made in haste are often decisions you live to regret. Always allow time to evaluate an investment before you commit your money.

taxes, while others do not. Not all intermediate-term investments provide exactly the same yield or exactly the same degree of safety. Thus, it is important to choose the investment that best fits your needs.

Characteristics of Intermediate-Term Investments

Current-income investments with intermediate maturities of from two to ten years have certain common characteristics with respect to yield, fluctuations in value, and liquidity. The common characteristics differentiate these investments from investments with short-term or long-term maturities. Understanding the characteristics that identify intermediate-term investments will allow you to determine whether they should be part of your investment portfolio.

Liquidity

Investments with maturities of two to ten years can generally be converted to cash on short notice, although you may suffer some loss of principal (that is, receive less than you paid), experience some sort of financial penalty, or pay a transaction fee. Intermediate-term investments have less liquidity than short-term investments such as money market funds, but there is more certainty regarding the amount of money to be received compared with investments that have maturities of twenty-five years and more. The liquidity of intermediate-term investments varies depending upon the type. A negotiable intermediate-term investment such as a corporate note can be liquidated before maturity only by selling the security to another investor, which nearly always involves a brokerage firm. The amount of money you receive depends on the price other investors are willing to pay, which may be more or less than you paid to acquire the investment.

Safety of Principal

The principal amount of most intermediate-term investments is quite safe—in many instances, totally safe. In other words, you can count on having the principal amount of the investment returned if you hold the investment to maturity. Absolute safety of principal is enjoyed by owners of U.S. Treasury securities and insured certificates of deposit. Notes issued by most federal agencies are generally considered to be only slightly less secure. Safety of principal for corporate notes varies from poor to very high depending both on the amount and quality of collateral that may be backing a particular note, and on the credit quality of the issuing firm. Even high-quality corporate notes do not have the safety of principal that is enjoyed by intermediate-term U.S. government securities.

Certainty of Income

In general, it is relatively certain that you will receive the income promised by intermediate-term investments, although certainty of income varies with the particular type of invest-

When evaluating investment companies, pay more attention to intermediate- and long-term performance rather than to short-term performance. The short-term investment performance of an investment company is often a poor indicator of the firm's future investment performance.

ment being considered. Notes issued and guaranteed by certain high-risk companies promise payments that are less than certain because the issuers may be subject to financial reverses that leave them unable to make the payments. At the opposite extreme, interest payments to the owners of U.S. Treasury securities are guaranteed by the U.S. government. Likewise, insured certificates of deposit provide investors with high certainty that income will be paid as promised.

Reinvestment Risk

Reinvestment risk—the risk that you may have to reinvest an investment's cash flow at a reduced yield—varies with the type of intermediate-term investment that is owned. Reinvestment risk is high when you must frequently reinvest large amounts of money. The larger the amount of money involved and the more frequently you must reinvest the money, the greater the amount of reinvestment risk. Investments that have maturities at the long end of intermediate-term range subject you to less reinvestment risk because you are seldom required to reinvest principal. Current income investments with maturities of two or three years subject you to substantial reinvestment risk because you must frequently reinvest principal at whatever yields prevail at the time funds are reinvested. Current-income payments also subject you to reinvestment risk if you anticipate that you will be reinvesting rather than spending the payments.

Stability of Value

Fluctuations in the values of current-income intermediate-term investments are primarily the result of changes in market interest rates. Rising interest rates cause a decline in the market values of outstanding current income investments such as U.S. Treasury, municipal, and corporate notes. Conversely, most current-income investments increase in value during periods of declining interest rates. Proportional changes in value vary directly with an investment's maturity length. Current-income investments with longer maturities are subject to greater price fluctuations. For example, securities with ten-year maturities, the long end of intermediate investments, fluctuate substantially more in value than securities with two-year maturities. Figure 11 compares the market values of two-year and eight-year fixed-income securities at various market interest rates (a 6-percent annual interest for the face amount is assumed for each security). Notice that the security with the longer maturity sells with a bigger premium at low interest rates and a bigger discount at high interest rates. Most certificates of deposit purchased by individual investors cannot be resold (that is, there is no secondary market) and, as a result, exhibit no fluctuations in value.

Current-income investments with short maturities are an appropriate choice if price stability is an important consideration. Remember, however, that price stability is a two-edged sword that does not produce the potentially higher yields that result from increases in value. Intermediate-term investments decrease more in value than short-term investments when market interest rates increase, but they also

If you plan to build a portfolio of bonds, stick to securities with a credit rating of A and above. Don't chase the higher yields offered by low-rated or nonrated bonds unless you are investing money you can afford to lose.

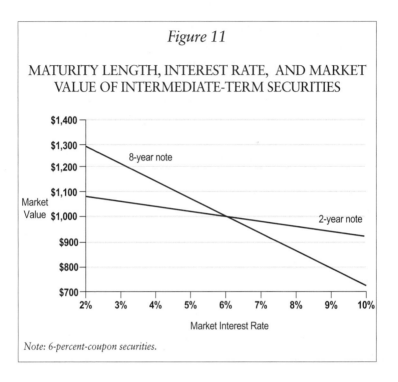

Figure 11

MATURITY LENGTH, INTEREST RATE, AND MARKET
VALUE OF INTERMEDIATE-TERM SECURITIES

Note: 6-percent-coupon securities.

produce bigger increases in value when market rates of interest decline. Fluctuations in market value caused by changes in market rates of interest should be of little concern if you are certain to hold an investment to maturity.

Yield

Current yields on intermediate-term investments generally fall between the higher yields from short-term investments and the lower yields on long-term investments. A direct relationship generally exists between yield and maturity length

---

Figure 12

YIELDS ON TREASURY SECURITIES OF DIFFERENT
MATURITY LENGTHS, AUGUST 1994

Maturity Length	Yield
Three months	4.5%
Six months	5.1
One year	5.6
Five years	7.0
Ten years	7.3
Twenty years	7.5

(see Figure 12). The yield curve described in Chapter 1 occasionally reverses, or "inverts," when short-term interest rates exceed long-term rates, but this is unusual and generally short-lived. The higher yields quoted on intermediate-term investments compared with short-term investments assume you will hold the investments to maturity. Intermediate-term investments sold before maturity may produce a loss in value that offsets all or a portion of the current yield.

Types of Intermediate-Term Investments

Several types of intermediate-term investments desirable for current income are readily available for purchase by individuals. The investments can be acquired through brokerage firms or directly from several types of financial institutions. Financial deregulation has resulted in individuals being able to acquire certificates of deposit from brokers, while U.S.

Treasury securities and municipal notes can be purchased through your local bank.

A debt security that remains outstanding has a maturity length that gradually becomes shorter. A twenty-five-year bond in ten years becomes a fifteen-year bond, and a fifteen-year bond eventually becomes a five-year bond. Corporate, municipal, and government bonds eventually assume the investment characteristics of notes regardless of the maturity lengths at the time the bonds were issued. A bond with a twenty-five-year maturity issued by General Motors twenty years ago has the same investment characteristics of a newly issued five-year note so long as the bond and the note have the same coupon, credit quality, and call feature. Despite the identical investment characteristics, bonds generally continue to be identified as bonds even when their maturity length falls below ten years.

U.S. Treasury Notes

U.S. Treasury notes have original maturities of from two to ten years and are direct obligations of the U.S. government. The U.S. Treasury regularly auctions notes with maturities of two, three, five, seven, and ten years. Notes with two-year maturities are auctioned monthly while securities with other maturities are issued quarterly. Once issued, Treasury notes are actively traded among dealers and investors in the over-the-counter market.

Unlike U.S. Treasury bills, discussed in the preceding chapter, but like most other forms of corporate and government debt, Treasury notes are *coupon securities* that pay semiannual interest. The combination of each security's coupon and face value determines the dollar amount of interest an investor receives each six months from the Treasury. For example, a $10,000 face amount U.S. Treasury note with a 6 percent coupon pays one-half of 6 percent of $10,000, or $300, in interest every six months until the note reaches maturity, at which time the face value is paid by the Treasury. The coupon rate is established at the time a note is issued and remains unchanged through the scheduled maturity.

U.S. Treasury notes may be purchased at the time of issue with either a competitive or noncompetitive bid directly through a Federal Reserve bank or indirectly through a brokerage firm or commercial bank. The notes are issued in $1,000 denominations but must be purchased at issue in minimum amounts of $5,000 and increments of $5,000. A competitive bid requires that you specify a price (determined by the yield you desire) that may or may not be accepted by the Treasury, depending on prices bid by other participants. Bidding too low a price (that is, requiring too high a yield) will result in your bid being rejected. A noncompetitive bid allows you to purchase new Treasury notes at the average price determined by competitive bidders. Competitive bidding is better left to big institutions that remain in close touch with the financial markets.

Treasury notes purchased by individual and institutional investors are subsequently traded in the secondary market and can be purchased through a brokerage firm or commer-

Treasury securities are not a bad deal, especially if you reside in a state with a relatively high income tax. Treasuries offer a combination of safety, liquidity, and tax benefits that are not enjoyed by any other investment.

cial bank. Notes in the secondary market may be purchased in units of $1,000 as opposed to the $5,000 multiples required when notes are purchased as part of a new issue. The focal point of the secondary market is a relatively small group of private securities dealers who provide continuous bid and offering prices.

The secondary market for Treasury notes is huge and offers a wide array of maturity lengths compared with the primary market, in which any particular auction offers a choice of only one or two maturities. The secondary market allows you to choose among all previously issued Treasury securities that remain outstanding. You are able to purchase a note that matures in a particular month of a particular year—an option that is unavailable in the primary market. For example, you can purchase a five-year note issued three-and-a-half years ago that has one-and-a-half years remaining to maturity. Daily price quotations for U.S. Treasury securities, such as the abbreviated list in Figure 13, are listed in many major metropolitan newspapers and the *Wall Street Journal*. Quotations are also easily obtained from brokerage firms.

The quotations in Figure 13 indicate each note's market value, price change, and yield during the afternoon of the previous day's trading. The quotation for the third note from the top indicates that the Treasury note with a 7 percent coupon and a September 1996 maturity last traded at a bid price of 101:13 and an asked price of 101:15. Treasury notes are traded in thirty-secondths of a point, a fraction that is indicated by the two digits to the immediate right of the colon. The bid represents the price at which a securities dealer is offering to purchase the note, in this case $101\frac{13}{32}$, which translates to $1,014.06 per $1,000.00 face amount. The note was being offered for sale at a price of $101\frac{15}{32}$, or

---

Figure 13

PUBLISHED PRICE QUOTATIONS
FOR U.S. TREASURY NOTES
(Partial Listing for August 18, 1994)

Rate	Maturity Mo/Yr	Bid	Ask	Chg.	Ask Yld.
4⅜	Aug 96n	96:18	96:20	- 6	6.21
7¼	Aug 96n	101:26	101:28	- 6	6.25
7	Sep 96n	101:13	101:15	- 6	6.30
8	Oct 96n	103:10	103:12	- 6	6.29
6⅞	Oct 96n	101:04	101:06	- 5	6.29
4⅜	Nov 96n	96:00	96:02	- 5	6.29
7¼	Nov 96n	101:27	101:29	- 8	6.32
6½	Nov 96n	100:10	100:12	- 6	6.32
6⅛	Dec 96n	99:20	99:22	- 5	6.27
8	Jan 97n	103:17	103:19	- 6	6.36
6¼	Jan 97n	99:22	99:24	- 7	6.36
4¾	Feb 97n	96:08	96:10	- 6	6.38
6¾	Feb 97n	100:24	100:26	- 6	6.40
6⅞	Mar 97n	101:02	101:04	- 6	6.40
8½	Apr 97n	104:28	104:30	- 7	6.44
6⅞	Apr 97n	100:31	101:01	- 7	6.45
6½	May 97n	100:00	100:02	- 7	6.47

$1,014.69, which is ⁵⁄₃₂ of a point lower (as indicated by the negative sign) than the asked price for this same note on the previous trading day. The note provides an annual yield to maturity of 6.30 percent based on the asked price. The lowercase *n* following the year of maturity indicates that the security was issued as a note rather than a bond. (Lack of this notation would mean that the security was issued as a Treasury bond.) Entries in the yield column creep gradually upward as maturities lengthen. The note with a September 1996 maturity has a yield to maturity of 6.30 percent, while the note with a May 1997 maturity—an increase in the maturity length of only eight months—provides a yield to maturity of 6.47. The yield is based on the assumption that notes purchased at the asked price will be held to maturity. Published prices and yields apply to transactions of $1 million and above. Transactions of less than $1 million require a slightly higher purchase price and result in a slightly lower selling price. Thus, purchasing the Treasury notes would cause you to realize slightly lower yields than those indicated in Figure 13.

Yield Current yields on U.S. Treasury notes are primarily a function of market interest rates. Treasury notes tend to yield more than Treasury bills but less than Treasury bonds. Current yields on all Treasury securities rise when market rates of interest increase and fall when market rates decline. Market interest rates, including yields on Treasury notes, can be expected to increase when investors anticipate substantial price inflation or when the Federal Reserve pursues a policy of restricted credit availability. Figure 14 illustrates annual yields on three-year and ten-year Treasury notes during the past three decades.

Treasury notes yield less than high-quality corporate

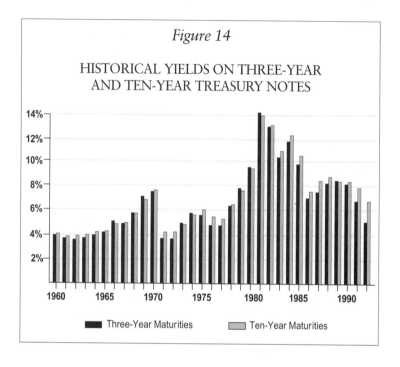

Figure 14

HISTORICAL YIELDS ON THREE-YEAR
AND TEN-YEAR TREASURY NOTES

notes of similar maturity, although yield differences between the two types of securities are often quite small. Treasury notes provide a lower yield partly because investors are willing to pay a premium price for securities with no credit risk (that is, interest and principal are certain to be paid). The notes have excellent liquidity and pay interest that is exempt from state and local income taxes—two factors that attract investors and produce lower yields.

Risk Treasury notes are essentially riskless with respect to interest and principal *so long as you hold the securities to maturity*. The U.S. government unconditionally guarantees scheduled payments. Outstanding notes fluctuate in value, however, and you will receive the existing market price should you liquidate your investment before maturity. An increase in interest rates since you purchased the notes is likely to cause you to have to sell at a price lower than you paid. A decline in interest rates will allow you to sell the notes for more than you paid. From the standpoint of knowing what price will be received in a sale (but not a redemption), Treasury notes entail less risk than either Treasury bonds or stocks, but more risk than the short-term investments discussed in the preceding chapter.

Summary: U.S. Treasury Notes Treasury notes provide the ultimate in credit quality with moderate price fluctuations. Interest income you receive is exempt from state and local taxation—an important advantage if you reside in a high-tax state such as California or New York. The current yields are nearly always significantly higher than those available on short-term investments but are somewhat lower than those earned on long-term investments, or even intermediate-term corporate notes. Still, U.S. Treasury notes can be a good investment choice if you are a conservative investor who demands safety of principal and interest but wants a yield that is higher than can be earned from money market funds and savings accounts.

Federal Agency Securities

Federal agency securities are debt of privately owned, publicly chartered government-sponsored agencies and of several federally related institutions, such as the Rural Electrification Administration, the Tennessee Valley Authority (TVA), the Export-Import Bank of the United States, the Small Business Administration, and the Government Na tional Mortgage Association (GNMA or "Ginnie Mae"). Federally related institutions are considered part of the federal government. Federally sponsored agencies include the Farm Credit Financial Assistance Corporation, the Federal Farm Credit Bank, the Federal Home Loan Bank, the Federal Home Loan Mortgage Corporation (Freddie Mac), the Federal National Mortgage Association (FNMA or "Fannie Mae"), the Financing Corporation, the Resolution Funding Corporation, and the Student Loan Marketing Association ("Sallie Mae"). Federally related institutions issued their own debt securities prior to 1973, but they currently borrow from a single source, the Federal Financing Bank. Debt securities issued before 1973 by the individual institutions continue to trade in the secondary market. Government-sponsored agencies currently issue their own securities.

Not all government-sponsored and federally related securities qualify as current-income debt with intermediate maturities. Most agencies have outstanding short-term and long-term debt, as well as intermediate-term debt. The Resolution Funding Corporation, which provides funding for the Resolution Trust Corporation, issues only debt securities with very long maturities. These instruments will eventually assume the investment characteristics of notes, but only after many years. Some agencies issue debt without a

---

Current-income investments are often a good choice for retirement accounts, especially if you already own a portfolio of investments such as common stocks and real estate with capital gains potential. Taxes on current income in a retirement account is deferred until withdrawal.

coupon at a discount from face value. And some agencies, including the Government National Mortgage Association and the Student Loan Marketing Association, also issue "participation securities," which are discussed in Chapter 4.

Federal agency securities are traded in the secondary market, where investors can purchase outstanding intermediate-term notes and bonds offered by dealers. Most issues are fixed-coupon securities that pay semiannual interest. An 8-percent-coupon, $10,000 FNMA debt security pays $400 of semiannual interest. The fixed coupon remains unchanged throughout a security's life and results in constant semiannual interest payments until maturity. Some agency issues are actively traded in the secondary market, while other securities have more limited trading. Liquidity should be an important consideration if you may need to sell a security prior to maturity. It is less important if you plan to hold your investment to maturity. A broker will be able to tell you which particular issues trade actively in the secondary market.

Agency securities are quoted in thirty-secondths of a point, the same as Treasuries. A quotation of 97:08 corresponds to a price of 97⅛₂, or 97.25 percent of face value. A $10,000-face-value agency security with this price quotation is trading for $9,725. Brokers will nearly always provide price and yield quotations that include the commission. Thus, you pay the quoted price, not the price plus a commission. Daily price quotations for federal-agency securities similar to the abbreviated list in Figure 15 are published in a limited number of major daily newspapers and in the *Wall Street Journal*.

The quotations for Federal National Mortgage Association debt securities illustrated in Figure 15 are virtually iden-

---

Figure 15

PUBLISHED PRICE QUOTATIONS FOR FNMA ISSUES
(Partial Listing for August 23, 1994)

Rate	Maturity	Bid	Asked	Yield
5.55	2-99*	93:26	94:02	7.13
7.50	3-99*	100:09	100:17	7.13
9.55	3-99	109:06	109:14	7.08
8.70	6-99	106:04	106:12	7.10
8.45	7-99	105:06	105:14	7.11
6.35	8-99	96:17	96:25	7.13
7.00	8-99*	99:00	99:08	7.18
8.55	8-99*	105:20	105:28	7.14
9.00	10-99*	99:26	100:02	8.98
8.35	11-99	104:19	104:27	7.21
8.65	12-99*	100:16	100:24	5.93
6.10	2-00	95:03	95:11	7.14
9.30	2-00*	101:00	101:08	6.47
9.05	4-00	108:00	108:08	7.24
9.80	5-00*	102:31	103:07	5.08
8.90	6-00	107:24	108:00	7.18

*Callable.

tical to the Treasury note quotations discussed previously. The coupon and maturity in the first two columns identify a particular security issue. Bid and asked price quotations indicate the prices being quoted by dealers to purchase (bid price) or sell (asked price) the security. The last column displays each security's yield to maturity or yield to call based on the asked price. Yield to call to the earliest call date (the date on which the security may be repurchased by the issuer prior to maturity at a predetermined price) is calculated for all callable agency securities—those with an asterisk to the right of the maturity date—selling above par. Yield to maturity is quoted for noncallable issues and for issues selling below par.

The seventh entry in Figure 15 is a 7-percent-coupon FNMA issue that matures in August 1999. Dealers are bidding $9,900 for each $10,000 of face value to buy the security and offering the security for sale at a price of 99%₂, or $9,925. The security is callable, but the current price is below 100 so the indicated annual yield of 7.18 percent is calculated as the yield to maturity, not the yield to call. As with Treasury quotations, the listed price quotations are for very large trades by institutional investors. You would pay a slightly higher price to purchase the notes and would receive a slightly lower price if you sold them.

Yield At any particularly time, current yields on federal agency securities are a function of current market rates of interest. Agency issues provide high yields when interest rates are high on certificates of deposit and fixed-income securities, and low yields during periods of low market rates of interest. Agency issues with intermediate maturities yield less than corporate notes but more than Treasury notes with equal maturities. Figure 16 compares yields provided by FNMA and U.S. Treasury notes on the same date.

Agency issues provide higher yields than Treasuries which are considered somewhat safer and offer potential tax benefits. Interest on Treasuries is exempt from state and local taxation (but not exempt from federal taxation), while interest income from most agency issues is fully taxable at the state, local, and federal level, the same as corporate

Figure 16

YIELD SPREADS FOR FNMA AND TREASURY NOTES OF SIMILAR MATURITIES
(Yields to maturity in late August 1994)

Maturity Length	FNMA Notes	U.S. Treasury Notes	Difference
Two years	6.34%	6.20%	.14%
Three years	6.61	6.55	.06
Four years	6.95	6.79	.16
Five years	7.13	6.90	.23
Ten years	7.53	7.32	.21

notes. Only debt issued by the Federal Home Loan Bank and the Federal Land Bank is exempt from state and local taxation. The yield spread between agency issues and direct Treasury obligations fluctuates and depends on investors' perceptions of the relative risk of agency issues. Investor concern about a particular agency's financial affairs will cause a widening of the yield premium.

Risk Most federal agency notes are guaranteed by the issuing agency, not the federal government. The credit quality of the notes is enhanced by the expectation that the federal government would come to the aid of a troubled agency that was having trouble meeting its financial obligations. The federal government may not be legally liable, but most individuals feel it is morally and practically liable for agency debts. The cost of borrowing for all federal agencies would increase substantially if one agency defaulted on its debt obligations. The implied federal backing of agency issues causes the notes to have somewhat more credit risk than Treasury issues, but credit quality similar to that on the very best corporate debt.

Agency issues fluctuate in market value, primarily because of changes in market rates of interest. The real value of your investment in an agency issue can also be consumed by unexpected inflation. The face value of the notes will be returned in ten years, but it may not buy a great deal. The relatively short maturities of most agency notes (as opposed to bonds) has a mitigating influence on both these risks. In general, federal-agency notes are a relatively low-risk investment. You won't get rich by investing in these securities, but you will probably earn a positive real return (a yield higher than the inflation rate) and it is unlikely you will lose any of your investment because of a default.

Summary: Federal Agency Securities Federal agency notes have a credit quality that is somewhat below Treasury securities but above most corporate debt. The payment of interest and principal is considered secure. Yields on agency notes are slightly higher than on Treasury notes of similar maturity but generally lower than on corporate notes. Agency notes are usually easy to resell and are a good investment choice for investors seeking current income with low risk.

Corporate Notes

Corporate notes are debt securities with original maturities of two to ten years. Most corporate notes pay semiannual interest until the security matures or is called by the issuer, at which time the owner of the debt receives the face value. Private businesses regularly issue large amounts of intermediate- and long-term debt that is available for purchase by individual investors. In addition, a huge amount of previously issued corporate debt is traded in the secondary market.

Corporate notes are issued and traded in $1,000 denominations. Most notes have fixed coupons, although some issues have variable coupons that fluctuate with short-term interest rates. The coupon and face value determine the amount of semiannual interest paid by the issuer. Prices of corporate notes and bonds are quoted as a percentage of face value (one point represents $10.00), with fractions in eighths of a point. Thus, a price of 98⅝ is 98.625 percent of $1,000.00, or $9,862.50. A half-point price change indicates that the price of a bond has changed by $5.00.

Many individual investors purchase ten, twenty-five, or more notes at a time, but no minimum number is required. A single $1,000 note can be purchased, although brokerage commissions are proportionately smaller on larger transactions. Selling small numbers of notes often results in a price penalty. Many corporate notes are traded on organized exchanges, while other issues are traded among dealers in the over-the-counter market. Corporate notes can be purchased as part of a new issue or from dealers in the secondary market. Brokerage commissions for new issues of corporate notes are paid by the issuer rather than by the buyer—an

---

Unless you need substantial amounts of current investment income to meet living expenses, try to assemble a balanced portfolio that offers the potential for capital gains as well as current income. Current-income investments suffer certain common risks that can only be reduced by acquiring different types of investments.

advantage to you. You are likely to pay a brokerage commission of $25 to $40 plus $5 per bond on purchases in the secondary market.

Most long-term corporate debt is issued with a call feature that permits the issuer to retire the securities at a predetermined price prior to maturity. The potential for a bond to be called is a disadvantage to an investor because the call is most likely to occur after interest rates have declined and the issuer can borrow at a lower rate of interest. At the same time, the investor who is forced to sell the bond back to the issuer would have to reinvest the proceeds at a lower return than that provided by the called bond. Many corporate notes are issued without a call feature, however, and you can hold them to the scheduled maturity.

Yield Although current yields on corporate notes are a function of prevailing market rates, they generally run higher than yields offered by agency and Treasury securities with equivalent maturities. The yield spread between corporate and Treasury notes results primarily from the higher credit risk of corporate securities. Debt with added credit risk can be sold only by offering investors higher yields. Corporate notes fluctuate in value, so your total yield may be different from the current yield if you purchase the note at other than face value or sell the note before maturity. In general, notes with longer maturities produce higher current yields and yields to maturity.

Risk Corporate notes and bonds have widely varying credit risk. The risk is a function of the financial strength of the issuer and the amount and quality of the collateral (if any) that the issuer has pledged as security. Adequate collateral can substantially reduce credit risk for the notes of a financially weak company. Notes of conservatively financed

Figure 17

CREDIT RATINGS OF CORPORATE AND MUNICIPAL DEBT

Duff and Phelps	Fitch	Moody's	Standard and Poor's	Description
1	AAA	Aaa	AAA	High-grade with extremely strong capacity to pay principal and interest.
2–4	AA	Aa	AA	High-grade by all standards but with slightly lower margins of protection.
5–7	A	A	A	Medium-grade with favorable investment attributes but some susceptibility to impairment with adverse economic changes.
8–10	BBB	Baa	BBB	Medium-grade with adequate capacity to pay interest and principal but possibly lacking certain protection against adverse economic conditions.
11–13	BB	Ba	BB	Speculative with moderate protection of principal and interest in an unstable economy.
14	B	B	B	Speculative and lacking desirable characteristics of investment bonds. Small assurance principal and interest will be paid on schedule.
15	CCC	Caa	CCC	In default or in danger of default.
16	CC	Ca	CC	Highly speculative and often in default or in danger of default.
17	—	C	—	Lowest rated class of bonds with extremely poor investment quality.
—	C	—	C	Income bonds on which no interest is being paid.
—	D	—	D	In default with principal or interest in arrears.

companies with good business prospects are high-quality, although a step below the credit quality of federal-agency and Treasury securities. Some corporate notes and bonds entail substantial uncertainty in regard to payment of interest and principal. Investors generally evaluate a note's credit risk according to the credit rating assigned by one or more of several credit-rating agencies.

Corporate notes subject investors to uncertainty about the price that will be received if the securities are sold before they mature. Like other fixed-income securities, corporate notes are subject to price fluctuations, caused primarily by interest rate changes. An investor is likely to suffer a loss on the sale of a note or bond if market rates of interest increase after the purchase date. Of course, you may be able to sell at a profit if interest rates decline. Lightly traded notes may elicit few offers and a low price in the event you wish to sell before maturity.

Summary: Corporate Notes Corporate notes with maturities of two to ten years generally offer fixed semiannual interest payments to a specified maturity date, at which time the face amount will be paid to the security holder. Compared to Treasuries, corporate notes offer higher yields at higher risk. Credit risk can be reduced by limiting your investments to securities with high credit ratings. Likewise, fluctuations in value can be reduced by purchasing securities with relatively short maturities. Because of fixed payments, long-term bonds subject investors to substantial purchasing-power risk.

Municipal Notes

Municipal notes are intermediate-term debt securities issued by states, counties, cities, and other political subdivisions,

Nearly all municipal debt is issued with a fixed coupon and semiannual interest payments that remain unchanged to maturity. A 5-percent-coupon municipal security with a $5,000 face value pays annual interest of $250 in $125 semiannual payments. Municipal debt is nearly always issued and traded in $5,000 denominations and $5,000 increments thereof. The relatively large denomination makes it difficult for some individual investors to purchase municipal securities.

Like corporate notes, municipal securities are issued through investment bankers who purchase the securities for resale to institutional and individual investors. The securities can be resold to dealers in the secondary market, although many municipal notes trade infrequently and a price penalty may be incurred on a sale, especially for a small trade. Municipal notes can be purchased from investment bankers as part of a new issue or from dealers who maintain portfolios of previously issued debt securities. Either type of transaction requires the services of a brokerage firm or commercial bank with access to the municipal securities market. If you are interested in purchasing municipal notes of a specific maturity issued by a certain city or state (say,

Don't buy investments over the telephone from someone you don't know, no matter how high the returns that are promised. Lots of unscrupulous individuals are out there trying to separate you from your money and they will go to any lengths to succeed. Invest your money only with reputable companies. If you have a question about a firm's reputation, call your local Better Business Bureau or write the Securities and Exchange Commission.

New York City notes maturing in 2004), the appropriate note is more likely to be available in the secondary market than in the primary market.

Municipal notes backed by the full taxing power of the issuer are termed *general obligation (GO) notes.* Notes backed only by the revenues of a particular project such as a toll road or a water-and-sewer system are termed *revenue notes.* The difference is important because GOs are generally of a higher quality.

Yield Yields on municipal notes are lower than yields on corporate and Treasury notes of similar risk and maturities. The lower yield results from the exemption of interest on most municipal notes from federal and, often, state taxation. Individuals who pay high tax rates can often earn higher *after-tax yields* by owning municipal notes than by owning federal or corporate securities. Municipal notes typically yield from 65 to 80 percent of the yield provided by taxable notes of similar maturity and credit quality.

Risk The credit quality of municipal notes varies over a wide range from very high to speculative. The credit quality of municipal notes is a function of the financial strength of the issuer. Most states and many cities, counties, and school districts issue notes of high quality. Many municipal issues are evaluated by the rating services mentioned in the above section on corporate notes and listed in Figure 17.

Like other fixed-income securities, municipal notes are subject to fluctuations in value caused by changes in market interest rates. The fluctuations are less than those of municipal bonds with longer maturities, and may be unimportant if you are certain to hold a note to its maturity. Municipal securities are discussed more fully in the next chapter.

Certificates of Deposit

A certificate of deposit (CD) is a savings certificate issued in return for a deposit of funds for a specific length of time, generally at a fixed rate of interest. For example, you may deposit $5,000 in a one-year CD that promises a return of 6 percent. Certificates of deposit are offered by savings and loan associations, commercial banks, and credit unions.

As part of a continuing effort toward financial deregulation (remember the resulting savings and loan debacle?), the government in 1983 allowed financial institutions the freedom to offer CDs in an infinite variety of amounts, maturities, and yields. The wide range of certificates doesn't mean that your local bank necessarily offers the exact CD you seek, however, since every institution does not ordinarily offer every option. You may be unable to locate a local institution that issues certificates with maturities of less than three months or more than ten years, for example. Each financial institution is free to establish its own restrictions and offer limited varieties of CDs with respect to amounts, maturities, and yields.

Certificates of deposit offer several advantages if you are a conservative investor seeking current income. The investments are generally safe from loss of principal or nonpayment of interest. They are offered locally, are not subject to fluctuations in market value caused by changes in market interest rates, and involve no transaction fees such as brokerage commissions. CDs also have some disadvantages. Interest income is fully taxable at both the federal and state level, and there is no possibility of gains in the value of the principal you invest. Certificates of deposit don't decrease in market value, but they also don't increase in value. Most institutions that issue CDs assess a penalty in the event you obtain your funds prior to maturity. You may also have to accept lower yields than you could earn by investing in high-quality fixed-income securities with similar maturities.

Insured certificates of deposit are also offered to individual investors by brokerage firms that negotiate yields with depository financial institutions. Higher yields are frequently available on these CDs compared with the yields you could earn by investing in CDs from local depository institutions. Brokered CDs are actually issued by banks and savings and loans and are marketed by the brokerage firms, which earn a fee from the issuing institution. Unlike CDs from your local bank, brokered certificates can be resold without penalty in a secondary market maintained by the brokerage firm, although these CDs sold prior to maturity are subject to the same market forces as publicly traded corporate and government notes. That is, a 6 percent CD sold in a market in which new CDs of similar maturity are being offered with a 7 percent yield will fetch less than the full principal amount of the CD. On the other hand, you should receive a premium if you sell a 7 percent CD in a market in which yields on new CDs are lower than 7 percent. Before investing in a brokered CD, make certain that the investment is purchased from a federally insured institution.

Obtain a copy of an investment company prospectus before investing your money. The prospectus describes a fund's investment goals and expenses, two items that should be crucial to your investment decision. The prospectus is available at no charge from the investment company (most have a toll-free telephone number) or from the brokerage firm selling the fund.

Yield Most financial institutions offer CDs with higher yields for larger deposits and longer maturities. Thus, a given institution is likely to pay a higher return on a $50,000 CD than on a $5,000 CD, and a higher return on a five-year CD than on a one-year CD. Yields on certificates of deposit vary with, but do not necessarily equal, the returns available on fixed-income investments with comparable maturities. Thus, yields on CDs increase during periods of rising interest rates, as depository financial institutions compete for funds with corporations, federal agencies, and the U.S. Treasury. Likewise, CD yields decline during periods of falling interest rates. In general, changing yields on CDs tend to lag changing yields on intermediate-term debt securities. Periods of rising interest rates typically produce CD yields that are lower than the returns that can be earned on corporate notes and even on agency and Treasury notes. Check the yields available on these other fixed-income investments before investing in a certificate of deposit or rolling the funds from a maturing CD into a new certificate.

Yields available on CDs of equal maturities often vary among institutions. Yields offered by an individual institution are in large part a function of that institution's need for funds. A bank with strong loan demand may pay 5½ percent on a five-year certificate at the same time that a bank with weak loan demand and a surplus of funds may pay only 5 percent on an otherwise identical CD. Differences in yield mean you should shop aggressively for the best rate. An extra half-percent annual return produces more than $500 in extra interest income over the life of a $20,000 five-year certificate of deposit.

Risk Certificates of deposit issued by financial institutions with federal insurance are very safe with regard to

Figure 18

CD YIELDS AT DEPOSITORY
FINANCIAL INSTITUTIONS IN ONE CITY

Institutions	Maturity Length					
	3 Mo	6 Mo	1 Yr	2 Yr	3 Yr	4 Yr
Credit union #1	3.70%	4.25%	4.89%	5.51%	5.77%	5.93%
Credit union #2	N/A	3.75	4.00	4.50	5.00	5.25
Credit union #3	3.55	3.56	4.07	4.59	4.85	N/A
Bank #1	3.82	4.07	4.70	5.12	5.38	5.64
Bank #2	3.40	3.90	4.35	5.15	5.15	5.27
Bank #3	3.29	4.00	4.50	5.00	5.50	5.75
Bank #4	3.40	3.95	4.50	5.25	5.40	5.40

Source: *Florida Times-Union* (Jacksonville), late August 1994.

payment of principal and interest so long as your total deposits in an institution do not exceed the $100,000 insurance limit established by the Federal Deposit Insurance Corporation (FDIC). Deposits exceeding the insurance limit are subject to loss in the event there is a collapse of the financial institution that issues the certificate.

CDs (other than brokered CDs) are not traded in the secondary market and thus are not subject to fluctuations in value. A penalty is generally assessed in the event you decide to cash in a CD prior to the scheduled maturity. Penalties are not mandated by the Federal Reserve and, as a result, vary from one institution to the next. A typical penalty involves an interest rate reduction to the rate paid on passbook savings accounts. An interest rate reduction caused by early withdrawal can prove to be a substantial monetary sacrifice. Be certain to inquire about an institution's policy for early withdrawal of funds from a certificate of deposit *before* you invest your funds. If there is a good chance you will require the funds in the near future, it is probably best to choose a CD with a shorter maturity even though the stated yield will be lower.

Summary: Certificates of Deposit Insured certificates of deposit are a safe alternative to publicly traded notes. Most CDs do not fluctuate in value but a penalty is generally imposed if you wish to obtain your funds before the scheduled maturity. Yields on these investments vary by size of investment, maturity, length, and issuing institution. You should compare the yields on certificates with yields on competing investments with comparable safety and maturity.

Establish an adequate emergency fund before you begin investing to meet long-term investment goals. An emergency fund is an important component of every individual's investment portfolio.

CHAPTER 4

Long-Term Investments That Provide Current Income

Many long-term investments—including corporate, municipal, and government bonds with long maturities, preferred stocks, certain common stocks, and pass-through certificates—produce large amounts of current income. The high current yields from these investments are offset, at least in part, by their greater risks compared with intermediate-term investments. Long-term assets are subject to relatively large fluctuations in value and the purchasing power of a lengthy stream of fixed income can be decimated by inflation. It is relatively difficult to judge the credit risk involved in long-term investments accurately.

Among investments that produce substantial amounts of current income, those with long lives tend to produce the most annual income and entail the greatest risks. If your choice of a long-term investment proves to be a good one, both with respect to the asset you select and the timing of the purchase, you are likely to make out like a bandit, earning substantial current income at the same time the investment increases in market value. A mistake with respect to timing or asset selection will make you wish you had kept your funds in an insured money market deposit account at the local bank or savings and loan.

Long-term assets are enticing investments for someone who is primarily interested in increased current income because the current yields on these investments are generally above the current yields on short- and intermediate-term investments. Twenty-five-year corporate bonds sometimes yield 3 or 4 percent more than one-year certificates of deposit. The higher yield that is generally available on long-term investments can produce substantial amounts of additional current income compared to an equal investment in a short- or intermediate-term investment.

Investing emulates most of life's other pursuits in that you don't get something for nothing. The higher current yields on long-term investments have a price, and the price is a higher risk from ownership. A variety of unfavorable

---

If short-term interest rates are higher than long-term interest rates, investors expect interest rates to fall. Keep this expectation in mind when you are deciding how long to sock away your money. Choosing a short-term investment will mean subsequent reinvestments are likely to be made at lower returns.

events can occur over a period of twenty to twenty-five years, and committing your funds at a fixed return for this length of time has the potential (but not necessarily the likelihood) for financial catastrophe. You may have a good feel for the business and economic climate a year from today, but how about twenty or thirty years down the road? How much purchasing power will inflation eat away over two decades? How about the financial health of the company that issued your preferred stock or the city that issued your bond? Most long-term investments can be sold, of course, but for how much? These and other important issues related to long-term investments are discussed in this chapter.

Characteristics of Long-Term Investments

Long-term investments that are desirable for the current income they produce have many of the same characteristics as intermediate-term investments, only the characteristics are exaggerated. Current yields are generally higher and changes in market value are greater. Compared to the investment characteristics of short-term assets, the characteristics of long-term investments are sufficiently different that the two groups of investments do not generally make good substitutes for each other. Long-term Treasury bonds are not good substitutes for Treasury bills and preferred stock is not a good substitute for a money market deposit account.

Liquidity

Individual long-term investments differ in respect to how easily they can be converted to cash, although, as a group, these investments tend to have substantially less liquidity than short-term investments and somewhat less liquidity compared to most intermediate-term investments. Some bonds and preferred stocks are seldom traded and may bring a reduced price in a sale, especially if you are in a hurry. The services of a broker are required to liquidate most long-term investments before maturity, so cashing in entails an expense. Some current-income investments are so long-term that there is no scheduled date on which your money will be returned. Preferred and common stocks do not have a maturity. You must pay a brokerage firm to sell shares of stock you own, even if the shares were purchased forty years earlier!

Some long-term investments are relatively easy to liquidate. Many stocks are actively traded and can be sold quickly without difficulty. Some, but not all bonds, are easily sold in the secondary market. Funds invested in a certificate of deposit can be withdrawn prior to the scheduled maturity, although some type of penalty will probably be assessed. The liquidity of individual long-term investments can generally be determined before you invest. If a long-term bond is actively traded today, you can generally expect that the bond will be actively traded in subsequent years, when you may be required to sell it. If there is a possibility that the investment may need to be sold quickly, liquidity should be an important consideration in your selection of a long-term investment.

Safety of Principal

Safety of the principal you invest in long-term assets can vary from very high to very low. The funds you invest in certain long-term investments are so secure there is virtually no chance you will lose any portion of your principal *so long as you hold the investment until the date your funds are scheduled to be returned.* You can be certain that funds invested in U.S. Treasury bonds will be returned on the scheduled maturity date. Likewise, high-grade corporate bonds offer excellent safety of principal. The principal amount of some other long-term assets is less secure. Long-term bonds are often issued and backed by financially weak companies and municipalities. Preferred stocks have a relatively weak guarantee of payment compared with secured bonds. The bottom line is that you must be very careful about where your funds are invested when a long-term commitment is involved.

Certainty of Income

Some long-term investments offer high certainty of income, while other investments may cause you to wonder from one period to the next whether the scheduled income will be paid. Certainty of income is closely related to an investment's safety of principal. Investments that offer substantial safety of principal can generally be counted on to make

Preferred stocks can be risky investments despite their name. In September 1994, USAir postponed dividends on all its preferred-stock issues, thereby reducing current income on these securities to zero. There was no assurance the postponed dividends would ever be made up. At the same time, USAir continued to make the required interest payments on its debt.

scheduled income payments. The face amount of a Treasury bond will be returned, just as the interest payments will occur as promised. On the other hand, both principal and interest payments are at risk when funds are invested in the bond of a financially weak organization. Long-term investments with unusually high yields are likely to have considerable uncertainty of income.

An investment on which income has been reduced or eliminated can be sold, but probably at a depressed price. As an investor interested in income-producing investments, how much would you pay for shares of ownership in a company that has been forced to eliminate its dividend, or bonds issued by a city that can no longer make the scheduled interest payments? Income investments that no longer pay income don't have a great deal of value in the secondary market.

Reinvestment Risk

Uncertainty of the return you will earn on reinvested cash flows is more important the larger the cash flows you are to receive and the sooner these flows are scheduled to occur. Owning an investment that produces large and frequent cash flows subjects you to substantial reinvestment risk. Long-term investments entail substantial reinvestment risk with respect to interest and dividend payments but relatively modest reinvestment risk with respect to the principal amount of the investment. Interest payments require frequent reinvestment, but the principal amount of a long-term investment may require reinvestment only every twenty or twenty-five years, depending on the maturity. A long-term bond will produce the same amount of semiannual income for twenty years or more without any need to reinvest the principal. Common and preferred stocks with no scheduled maturity require no reinvestment of principal.

Stability of Value

The market values of long-term investments are less stable than those of intermediate-term investments and substantially less stable than those of short-term investments. Fluctuating values of long-term investments with high current yields result mostly from changes in market interest rates. A large increase in interest rates has a depressing effect on the market value of a long-term investment that produces current income. The longer the maturity, the bigger the decline. Consider being locked in to a 6-percent coupon, twenty-year U.S. Treasury bond when newly issued bonds are being sold with 9-percent coupons. As owner of the Treasury security you will receive twenty years of $60 annual interest payments, $30 less than you would receive from one of the new 9 percent bonds. Of course, lack of price stability can work in your favor because the market value of bonds increases as well as decreases. Hold an income-producing asset with a long maturity during a period of declining interest rates and you will have a gold mine.

Most long-term investments desired for the current income they produce are subject to relatively small amounts

Treasury bills sometimes offer significantly higher yields than money market funds or money market deposit accounts. If you carry a large balance in either of the latter two investments, check out the yields that are available on U.S. Treasury bills.

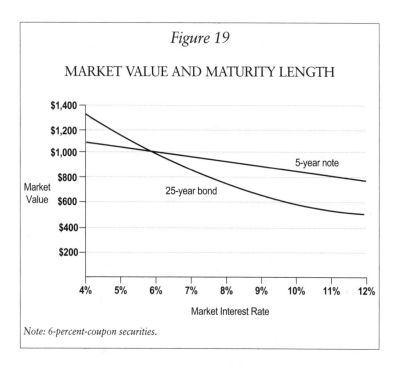

Figure 19

MARKET VALUE AND MATURITY LENGTH

Note: 6-percent-coupon securities.

of market risk. That is, the market values of these invest-ments are not subject to large random fluctuations. The price of stocks, even the high-dividend variety, is subject to market fluctuations, even during periods of stable interest rates. Infrequently traded preferred stocks and bond issues can be subject to unusually large price movements.

Yield

The current yield (yield from current cash payments) on long-term assets is generally somewhat higher than the cur-rent yield on intermediate-term assets and substantially higher than the yield on short-term assets. While a money market account may yield 3 percent, and a five-year Treasury note yield 5½ percent, preferred stocks and long-term bonds may yield 7 percent. The current yield on long-term assets is higher than the yield on intermediate- and short-term assets so long as the yield curve remains upward sloping, the curve's normal shape.

Although this book concentrates on current income, total returns are also important, especially when long-term investments are being considered. The two measures of return are the same for most short-term investments, but changes in market values of long-term investments may result in very different total and current returns. Declining market values can cause the total yield on a long-term asset to be lower than the total yield you would have earned on an intermediate- or short-term asset. Suppose you purchase a long-term bond with a current yield of 8 percent and the bond declines 10 percent in value during the first year of ownership. The total yield for the first year is minus 2 percent (an 8 percent return from interest income and a negative 10-percent return from the change in value). You could have earned a higher total return by choosing to leave your money in a regular savings account. In this instance, you would have been better off keeping the funds in a coffee can.

Long-term investments also experience increased market values that can cause total returns to be much higher than current returns. A 7-percent coupon, twenty-year corporate bond purchased prior to a major decline in market interest rates will produce $70 in annual interest income at the same time the bond experiences a substantial increase in market value. The additional return from the increase in market value adds to the higher current yield on the bond compared with the return you would have earned from a money market deposit account.

Types of Long-Term Investments

Several long-term investments are desirable primarily for the current income they produce. Even though you are willing to incur the risks inherent in a long-term investment, you must determine which particular type of investment best meets your needs. Should you purchase a long-term corporate bond because the yield is higher than on a U.S. Treasury bond of equal maturity? Is it better to choose preferred or common stocks rather than bonds? If you decide to invest in shares of stock, should you go with preferred stock or would you be better off owning common stocks with high dividend payments?

Common Stocks

Common stocks represent ownership units, or *shares* in a business. Common-stock ownership gives investors a claim to the profits of the business. Some businesses issue only a few shares of ownership, while other businesses issue tens or hundreds of millions of shares to investors, who supply the businesses with money to acquire buildings, machines, and items to sell. The more shares of a business that are outstanding, the less the value of each share. Investors who purchase shares of common stock often subsequently resell the shares in the secondary market to other investors. The common shares of some companies are listed for trading on an organized securities exchange such as the New York

Stock Exchange or the Pacific Stock Exchange. Other stocks trade in the over-the-counter market.

Profits a business earns can be retained and used to reduce debt or acquire additional assets, or can be paid as dividends to the firm's stockholders. The portion of earnings paid in dividends is known as the *dividend payout ratio*. Growing companies often retain all or a large portion of their earnings (that is, they have a low payout ratio) because of the need to spend large sums of money on new plants and additional inventories. Stockholders receive nominal dividends but anticipate their ownership shares will increase in value as the companies expand in size and earn higher profits. Growing profits generally lead to higher dividends. Thus, a low dividend payout ratio facilitates a company's growth and improves the likelihood of higher dividends in future years. Stocks with low dividend payout ratios may offer the potential for substantial growth in value, but the low dividend makes these stocks inappropriate for investors seeking current income.

Companies with limited growth prospects have less need to reinvest profits and they pay most of their profits as dividends to their stockholders. Although companies seldom distribute all of their earnings as dividends, firms sometimes allocate 60 to 80 percent of earnings to dividend payments. Higher dividends mean less earnings available for reinvestment in new assets and generally result in lower earnings

Income stocks offer the potential of increased dividend payments, although annual increases are generally small. Still, any increase is to be preferred over the fixed interest stream that is available on most debt securities.

Figure 20

EARNINGS, DIVIDENDS, AND PAYOUT RATIOS

Company	Earnings per Share	Dividend per Share	Dividend Payout	Share Price	Dividend Yield
Albertson's	$1.39	$ .36	25.9%	$26	1.4%
American Greetings	1.77	.48	27.1	30	1.6
Amoco	3.52	2.20	62.5	59	3.7
Anheuser-Busch	3.55	1.36	38.3	52	2.6
Caterpillar	3.36	.30	8.9	54	0.6
Chrysler	6.77	.60	8.9	47	1.3
Goodyear	3.23	.53	16.4	37	1.4
Green Mountain Power	2.20	2.11	95.9	29	7.3
Nichols Research	1.13	—	—	12	—
Pepsico	1.96	.61	31.1	31	2.0
Procter & Gamble	2.82	1.10	39.0	54	2.0
Ryder System	1.53	.60	39.2	25	2.4
Del Webb	1.05	.20	19.0	17	1.2
Westinghouse	.76	.40	52.6	14	2.9

Note: Data for fiscal year 1993; share prices from late summer 1994.

and dividend growth in future years. Limited growth prospects, in turn, cause many investors to shun a company's common stock, thereby penalizing the stock's market value. The combination of limited growth prospects, a high dividend payout ratio, and a low stock price produces a stock that competes with bonds for the funds of investors seeking high levels of current income. Common stocks with high dividends relative to their respective stock prices (that is, a high dividend yield) are called *income stocks*.

A company's dividend policy is established by the firm's directors, who, technically at least, are representatives of the common stockholders. Directors meet periodically, usually quarterly, and decide on the amounts and dates for upcoming dividends. Most companies pay dividends quarterly, although some make semiannual or annual payments. Thus, a company that pays common stockholders $4.40 per share in annual dividends will make quarterly payments of $1.10. Companies sometimes issue several classes of common stock, although this is the exception rather than the rule. Most firms have only a single type of common stock outstanding.

Following the quarterly dividend meeting, directors publicly announce information regarding the upcoming dividend. For example, directors may announce on December 5 that the firm will pay a dividend of 25 cents per share on January 12 to stockholders of record on December 27. As a stockholder of record on December 27, you will receive the January 12 dividend payment *even though you may no longer own the stock on January 12*. December 27 is the crucial date that determines who will receive the dividend payment. Dates relevant to a dividend are summarized in Figure 21. Companies typically pay dividends on the same dates each year unless a scheduled date is a weekend or holiday.

The purchase or sale of common stock generally requires

Common-stock dividends are one of the first payments to be reduced or eliminated when a company encounters serious financial difficulty. Common stocks are relatively risky investments when investment income is required to meet current living expenses.

Figure 21

RELEVANT DIVIDEND DATES

announcement date The date on which a corporation's directors publicly announce the amount and relevant dates of the upcoming dividend. Also called *declaration date*.

ex-dividend date The first date a buyer of the stock will *not* receive the dividend. A stockholder must purchase stock at least one day before the ex-dividend date to receive the next dividend. The ex-dividend date is four business days prior to the date of record.

record date The date on which a stockholder must be registered on the books of the company to receive the next dividend. The date of record is established on the announcement date. Also called the *date of record* and the *stockholder-of-record date*.

payment date The date on which dividend checks are mailed or credited to stockholders. Many companies offer an option that allows stockholders to have dividends wired to a bank account on the payment date.

Relevant dividend dates for Cincinnati Bell, Inc.

Declaration Date	Ex-dividend Date	Record Date	Payment Date	Per-share Amount
Feb 7, 1994	Mar 31, 1994	Apr 6, 1994	May 2, 1994	$ .20
Jun 6, 1994	Jun 30, 1994	Jul 6, 1994	Aug 1, 1994	$ .20
Sep 6, 1994	Sep 29, 1994	Oct 5, 1994	Nov 1, 1994	$ .20
Dec 12, 1994	Dec 29, 1994	Jan 4, 1995	Feb 1, 1995	$ .20

the services of a brokerage company that charges a commission. Only a small number of companies sell their own shares directly to the public without a commission. Commissions vary among brokerage firms, so it pays to shop around. Brokerage firms that offer investment advice typically levy the highest charges, which may be two or three times the commissions charged by discount brokerage firms.

Commission charges should be an important consideration in choosing a brokerage firm, especially if you feel comfortable selecting which stocks to purchase.

Yield Owners of common stock receive current income only from dividend payments. Gains or losses in stock value affect total yield but not current yield. Current yield for common stock is calculated by dividing a stock's current market price into the annual dividend. Thus, Exxon common stock that trades on the New York Stock Exchange for $60.00 per share with an expected annual dividend of $3.00 per share has a current yield of $3.00/$60.00, or 5.0 percent. A stock's current yield changes as the stock price or dividend changes. If Exxon stock subsequently increases in price to $70.00 per share but the dividend remains unchanged, current yield will fall to $3.00/$70.00, or 4.3 percent.

Current yield for common stocks, even stocks that qualify as income stocks, is generally below yields that are available on bonds and preferred stocks. Income stocks at least offer the potential for increased dividends that would result in a higher income and produce a higher current yield for investors who purchased shares at the current price. Suppose a common stock currently selling for $25.00 pays a $1.00 annual dividend—a current dividend yield of 4 percent. A subsequent increase in the dividend to $1.20 will

---

Always check the quality rating of a bond or a preferred-stock issue before you put money into one of these investments. Quality ratings by the credit-rating agencies are good indicators of how likely you are to receive promised income payments. Most public and college libraries subscribe to one or more of the financial services that provide this information.

produce a higher current yield based on the current market price of the stock. The stock may also increase in price, allowing current owners to enjoy a total yield higher than the current dividend yield. The potential for dividend growth, however small, often causes income stocks to sell at prices that produce relatively modest current yields. If investors are fairly certain a company's dividend will not increase, the current dividend yield on the firm's common stock should approximately equal the current yield on medium-grade long-term corporate bonds.

Risk Common stocks are among the riskiest of the long-term investments that are desirable for the current income they produce. Dividends to common stockholders are not guaranteed and are dependent on a company's profits. Dividend payments to holders of common stock are subordinate to the claims of employees, directors, suppliers, the Internal Revenue Service creditors, and preferred stockholders. These other claims are sometimes so large that little or nothing is left for common stockholders, who may find their dividend income reduced. Companies find it much easier to reduce or eliminate the dividend to owners of common stocks than to reduce interest payments to creditors.

Changes in market interest rates cause common stock prices to fluctuate. Stock has no maturity date so no date is scheduled for the return of your principal. The infinite life causes the values of income stocks to be affected by changes

Don't invest too large a proportion of your funds with a single financial institution or in a single issue. Even the most secure government or private institution can encounter unexpected financial difficulties that place your funds at risk.

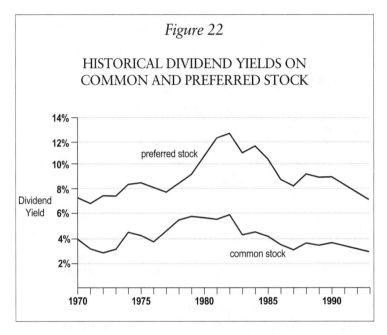

Figure 22

HISTORICAL DIVIDEND YIELDS ON
COMMON AND PREFERRED STOCK

in market interest rates in much the same manner as the values of bonds with very long maturities. Rising interest rates have a negative effect on the prices of income stocks and falling interest rates cause the income stocks to rise in price.

Summary: Common Stocks Common stocks with high dividend payments have the advantage of potential increases in dividend income. Dividend increases depend on future profitability of the underlying business. On the negative side, dividends are not guaranteed and are subject to being reduced or eliminated. A reduced dividend may result in a substantial decline in the market value of a common stock, especially if the dividend cut is unexpected. Common stocks are riskier investments than debt securities of the same company. Income stocks can play a role in a current-income portfolio, but they should be balanced with both short- and intermediate-term debt.

Preferred Stock

Preferred stock designates a special type of business owner-ship that has priority over common stock with respect to dividends and assets. Preferred stockholders have a claim that is junior to the claims of creditors. Dividends to preferred stockholders are generally fixed in dollar amount and paid in equal quarterly installments. A limited number of preferred stock issues pay dividends that are keyed to some variable, often a specific short-term interest rate. A share of preferred stock is analogous to a perpetual cash machine that spits out quarterly checks for a fixed amount of money, much as a bond pays a fixed amount of semiannual interest. The amount of the dividend is established at the time the stock is issued and may be stated as an annual dollar amount or as a percentage of par value. The par value of individual stock is-sues varies, but is usually $10, $50, or $100. Thus, a 6 per-cent $100 preferred stock pays a per-share quarterly dividend of $1.50 ($6.00 per year). Many companies issue no pre-ferred stock while other firms have several outstanding issues of preferred. Utilities are major issuers of preferred stock.

Preferred stock is in certain respects like perpetual debt (that is, debt without a maturity). Most preferred shares generate fixed payments and, like common stock, have no maturity date on which the principal must be repaid by the issuer. On the other hand, an owner of preferred stock is not a creditor and does not have a legal right to dividends. Divi-dends to holders of preferred stock may be discontinued if a company encounters severe financial difficulties, although missed dividends on most issues of preferred must eventually be brought up to date before the company can pay any dividends to common stockholders.

A major disadvantage of owning preferred stock is the absence of any possibility to participate with other owners in the increasing profits of a successful business. The annual dividend to preferred stockholders is generally fixed and will not increase regardless of how profitable the company becomes. If the firm becomes a takeover target of another firm (that is, if another business attempts to become the owner by offering to purchase the shares of the current owners), common stockholders will make a bundle while you, as a preferred stockholder, are unlikely to receive more than the face value of the stock you own. Like bonds, preferred stock will increase in market value during a period of declining interest rates.

Yield The current yield to preferred stockholders is calculated in the same manner as for common stockholders. That is, current yield equals the annual dividend divided by the market price of the stock. Shares with a $3.50 annual dividend and a $50.00 market price provide a current yield of $3.50/$50.00, or 7 percent. The current yield of any preferred stock changes constantly as the market price of the stock fluctuates. Fluctuations in the market value of pre-

---

Annuities sold by insurance companies often include heavy commissions and expenses that can penalize your return, especially if you decide to liquidate the investment after only four to five years. On the other hand, annuities offer certain tax advantages and can be a good investment if you are investing to achieve long-term goals.

Figure 23

SELECTED PREFERRED-STOCK ISSUES

Issue	Annual Dividend	Market Price	Dividend Yield
Alabama Power A	$1.90	$23¼	8.2%
Atlanta Gas Light	1.93	24⅛	8.0
BankAmerica A	3.25	46	7.1
Bethlehem Steel	5.00	52	9.6
Cleveland Electric	7.40	71	10.4
Digital Equipment	2.22	22¼	10.0
Ford Motor B	2.06	25⅛	8.2
General Motors D	1.98	24¾	8.0
Georgia Power S	1.93	24	8.0
Illinois Power G	4.12	50½	8.2
Mascotech	1.20	15	8.0
Norfolk Southern	2.60	37¼	7.0
Olin A	3.64	51⅝	7.1
Republic New York C	1.94	24⅛	8.0
Sears	2.22	25⅛	8.8
Texaco B	1.60	24¼	6.6
Westinghouse	1.53	15½	9.0

Note: Prices and dividend yields are as of late September 1994. Long-term corporate bonds of medium quality were yielding approximately 8.9 percent at this time.

Letters following company names identify the preferred-stock series of the issuer.

ferred shares cause investors to earn total returns that may be higher or lower than current yields.

At any particular time, current yields available on individual issues of preferred stock are dependent on the level of long-term interest rates and the riskiness of the dividend stream. In general, the current dividend yield on high-quality preferred stocks is related to and somewhat higher than the yield to maturity on investment-grade bonds with long maturities. If the long-term debt of General Motors yields 8 percent, the firm's preferred stock will generally provide a slightly higher current yield.

Preferred stock is more risky than debt securities of the same company and should provide a higher yield. Creditors own a higher-priority claim to a company's income and assets than do preferred stockholders. Nevertheless, an available tax break on dividend income earned by businesses causes companies to bid aggressively for preferred stock (a large proportion of dividend income is free from corporate but not personal income taxes). The demand from businesses pushes preferred-share prices up and current yields down. Individual investors who don't enjoy the same tax break are often unable to earn a current yield that is sufficient to justify the risks of investing in these securities.

Risk Certain investment risks apply to all preferred stock while other risks are peculiar to individual issues. Fixed dividend payments cause the market values of preferred shares to fluctuate inversely with market rates of interest. Falling interest rates result in rising preferred-stock prices, while interest rate increases cause price declines in virtually all preferred stocks. The lack of a maturity date causes interest rate risk to be somewhat greater for holders of preferred stock than for the owners of long-term bonds.

Bond investments offer a wide range of maturity lengths, which allow you to minimize the effect of interest rate changes.

The infinite maturity and fixed dividend payments inherent in preferred-stock investments also result in substantial purchasing-power risk from unexpected inflation. Annual dividend income of $3,500 from a $50,000 investment in a 7 percent issue of preferred stock currently has substantial purchasing power. The same investment income twenty years from now will almost certainly purchase much less. An investment with fixed payments will prove to be a disastrous choice if higher-than-anticipated inflation eats away most of your purchasing power.

The risk of not receiving promised dividend payments varies with individual issues of preferred stock. Financially weak companies may find it very difficult to meet the dividend requirements of preferred-stock issues. A cessation of dividend payments will generally cause a major decline in a stock's market value (unless it is widely expected), causing you to receive a depressed price in the event you decide to sell the shares. Over a period of years or decades, even financially strong companies can encounter unforeseen difficulties that leave them in financial straits. Investors' perceptions that a company's operating and financial condition is deteriorating is likely to cause a decline in the market value of the firm's preferred stock.

Summary: Preferred Stocks Preferred stocks are similar to bonds with an infinite life, only without most of the debt securities' safeguards. Fixed payments to holders of preferred stock have priority only over the payments made to common stockholders. All payments to employees, suppliers, and creditors have priority over the payments promised to owners of preferred stock. The low ranking of preferred-stock payments relative to other corporate obligations makes preferred stock a relatively risky security to own. The risk is particularly relevant considering that owners of preferred stock do not directly participate in a firm's success. The same fixed payments continue regardless of how much profit the issuer earns, unless profits disappear, in which case dividends may be discontinued.

The bottom line is that you can probably earn a similar yield at less risk by investing in long-term bonds. Bonds have priority with regard to payments and a maturity date designates when the face value of the bond will be returned. If you decide to invest in shares of preferred stock, be sure to choose an issue that is *cumulative*. Dividends on cumulative preferred stock must be current (that is, any missed dividends must be made up) before any dividend payments can be made to the firm's common stockholders.

Annuities

An annuity is an insurance contract that provides regular income payments. Any stream of fixed payments is technically an annuity. Quarterly dividends to preferred stockholders and semiannual bond interest payments are both examples of annuities. Interest payments from certificates of deposit also qualify as annuities. Retirement benefits from an employer are generally in the form of an annuity with equal monthly payments for life. More specifically, insurance companies sell annuities as investment vehicles. Most insurance company annuities are fixed and provide a constant periodic income for a specified period or for a person's lifetime. Insurance companies also sell variable annuities whose payments vary with the value of a group of investments, usually common stocks. An annuity can be purchased with a single large payment or with a series of payments over many years. *Immediate annuities* begin making payments at the time of purchase, while *deferred annuities* begin payments on some specified future date. Owning an annuity makes you an *annuitant*.

Annuities are ordinarily purchased as vehicles to fund retirement, but they can also serve as an investment to supplement employment income. In this respect annuities compete with other fixed-income investments mentioned in this book. You can acquire additional income by investing in annuities as well as by putting your funds in stocks and bonds. Unlike dividend and interest payments from stocks and bonds, annuity payments are comprised both of interest and principal. That is, each annuity payment consumes a portion of your investment principal. The result is analogous to selling a portion of your bond or stock portfolio each period in order to supplement your interest or dividend income.

Several types of annuities are available for purchase. Certain annuities guarantee only a limited number of payments. For example, you can purchase an annuity that pays $400 per month for ten years. Payments would be discontinued at the end of this period. Alternatively, you could select an annuity with payments that last twenty years or twenty-five

Fixed-income investments with long maturities (thirty-year bonds, for example) are subject to great risk from unexpected inflation. Inflation over many years can eat away a large proportion of the purchasing power of the interest income and principal. Inflation is difficult to forecast, especially for long periods.

years. The longer the period over which payments are scheduled, the smaller the payment size or the greater the cost of the annuity. Likewise, annuities are most costly the larger the payment you are to receive. An annuity that pays $600 per month costs approximately twice as much as an annuity that pays $300 monthly. (Equivalent administrative expenses may cause the larger annuity to cost slightly less than twice as much.)

Life annuities—fixed payments for as long as you live— can be a good investment choice if you desire a guaranteed monthly income without the worry if outliving your capital. Annuities are also available that guarantee you and some other individual (your spouse, usually) an income for as long as either of you lives. Insurance companies price life annuities on the basis of an annuitant's life expectancy. The longer your life expectancy, the more you must pay for an annuity of a given size or the smaller the annuity payments you must accept for a given cost. The younger you are when annuity payments are scheduled to begin, the more the insurance company will charge for the annuity.

Yield Yields you earn from an annuity are a function of the returns the insurance company expects to earn from investing the premiums you pay. Periods of high interest rates generally result in strong earnings projections that cause insurance companies to offer high returns and generous annuity payments. Interest earned on both principal and accumulated interest builds up within the annuity free from current income taxes; the taxes must be paid at the time payments are received from the insurance company. High yields on certificates of deposit, bonds, and preferred stocks also produce a competitive environment in which insurance companies must offer high yields to attract your business.

Conversely, low market rates of interest reduce insurance company returns and reduce the yields you can earn on alternative investments.

Returns on annuities are approximately equal to the returns you can earn on high-quality bonds with intermediate- to long-term maturities. Yields vary, so compare the offerings of several insurance companies. Insurance companies each have different expenses and investments, and this causes them to offer annuities with different returns. Remember, however, that annuity payments are comprised of both investment income and principal. The combined amounts produce annuity payments that exceed interest or dividend payments you would receive from investing an equal amount of money in bonds or stocks, respectively.

Risk Annuity payments are guaranteed by the insurance company that sells the annuity. Thus, the safety of your investment is a function of the financial stability of the insurance company. Payments may be endangered if the insurance company encounters financial difficulties because of unwise investment selection or lack of cost controls. Insurance companies are regulated by the states in which they operate rather than by the federal government. No federal guarantees back your annuity payments although some states provide limited guarantees that augment insurance company promises. Still, there are risks to owning annuities so it is important to investigate the financial stability of an insurance company carefully before purchasing an annuity from it.

The fixed payments of an annuity suffer the same purchasing-power risk as preferred stocks and long-term bonds. A period of unexpectedly high inflation will seriously erode the purchasing power of annuity payments. Monthly payments of $2,000 may seem like a substantial amount of money now, but how much will the same payments buy in another ten or twenty years? Think how much more purchasing power this same amount of money had ten or twenty years in the past.

Summary: Annuities An annuity can be a good investment choice for someone who wants to maximize current income and isn't concerned about capital gains. Annuities are generally used to supplement retirement income but can be purchased at any age. You can choose an annuity that makes a specific number of payments or that guarantees payments for your lifetime. Annuity investments are subject to certain risks that are related to both the credit quality of the insurance company that guarantees the payments and the purchasing power of the payments to be received. Unlike marketable securities such as bonds and preferred stocks, annuities cannot be resold and do not fluctuate in value.

Mortgage Pass-through Securities

Mortgage pass-through securities, also called *pass-throughs* or *certificates of participation,* are shares of ownership in specific collections, or pools, of mortgages. Some pools contain only fixed-rate mortgages and other pools contain only variable-rate mortgages. Borrowers' monthly mortgage payments, including interest, principal, and prepayments to lenders are "passed through" (hence, the name) to certificate owners, after being reduced somewhat by fees to service and guarantee the mortgage payments.

Pass-throughs are issued and guaranteed by three different federal agencies: the Federal Home Loan Mortgage Corporation (Freddie Mac), the Federal National Mortgage Association (Fannie Mae), and the Government National Mortgage Association (Ginnie Mae). Pass-throughs are also issued by private financial institutions such as savings and loan associations and commercial banks. The organizations pool and sell participation certificates to generate fee income for themselves and to raise capital that can be used to make additional mortgage loans. The certificates provide an opportunity for income-oriented investors to earn the relatively high current yields that are generally available on mortgage loans.

Ginnie Mae issues two types of certificates, one secured by fixed-rate mortgages and the other by variable-rate mortgages. Payment of principal and interest on both types of pass-throughs are fully backed by the U.S. government, which results in Ginnie Mae pass-throughs having no credit risk. Freddie Mac pass-throughs are also issued against pools of fixed-rate mortgages and pools of adjustable-rate mortgages. Pass-throughs from Freddie Mac are not backed by the full faith and credit of the U.S. government, although the certificates are considered to be high-quality securities. Fannie Mae pass-throughs (alternatively called *mortgage-backed securities*) are also high-quality but not directly backed by the credit of the U.S. government. Like Freddie Mac, Fannie Mae issues certificates backed by pools of fixed-rate mortgages and pools of variable-rate mortgages.

Participation certificates generally pass through to investors whatever payments are made on the underlying mortgages (less service charges). The principal amount of a certificate is reduced as principal is repaid on the underlying mortgages. A certificate backed by thirty-year mortgages is likely to be repaid much sooner than thirty years, as many borrowers prepay their loans when they sell their homes or refinance their existing mortgages. Your problem as a certificate holder is not knowing for certain how much money you will be receiving each month. If mortgage interest rates fall and large numbers of homeowners refinance their mortgages you will receive unusually large principal payments. Rapid repayment of principal will cause a reduction in subsequent interest payments you receive. On the other hand, homeowners will not refinance and may even hesitate to move to a new home when market rates of interest increase. An increase in market rates of interest causes the monthly payments to an owner of a pass-through certificate to be smaller and occur over a longer period of time than expected.

Yields Pass-through certificates provide some of the highest yields and cash flows that are available from a high-quality investment. It is not unusual for pass-throughs to yield 1 to 2 percent above the yield on long-term Treasury securities. Yields available on these certificates depend primarily on the level of long-term interest rates. Current yields on pass-through certificates are relatively high during periods of high long-term rates and low during periods of low interest rates. Pass-through certificates are traded in the secondary market and are subject to changes in market value that can affect the total yield you earn from them. For example, if you purchase a certificate backed by thirty-year mortgages and long-term market rates of interest subsequently decline, you can expect the market value of your certificate to increase. If you plan to hold your investment until mortgages backing the certificate have been completely repaid, changes in the market value of the certificate will be of no consequence and you will earn the quoted yield at the time the investment was purchased.

Collateralized mortgage obligations (CMOs) are debt securities backed by mortgage-related securities such as pass-throughs. Pools of mortgages back pass-through certificates, while pools of pass-through certificates back collateralized mortgage obligations. CMOs were developed to reduce the uncertainty of pass-through prepayments by directing certain payments to various groups of bonds issued against the pass-throughs. Thus, CMOs of different maturities are developed from a single pool of pass-throughs. Early prepayments are directed to CMOs with short maturities and subsequent prepayments go to owners of CMOs with longer maturities. CMOs add another level of fees to service the securities.

Risk Pass-throughs have high credit quality. You know interest and principal will be paid, you just don't know when. In general, pass-throughs produce very large cash flows during periods of falling interest rates, when you would prefer to receive small payments. The opposite occurs during periods of rising interest rates. The potential for rapid repayment of principal causes pass-through certificates to have considerable reinvestment risk. Different certificates have different likelihoods for accelerated payment streams. Participation certificates in mortgages with high interest rates will be repaid quickly because homeowners with high-interest loans are most likely to prepay their mortgages. Thus, you have some control over the rate of repayment by your choice of the particular certificate you purchase.

Pass-through certificates traded in the secondary market fluctuate in value as market interest rates and investor risk perceptions change. Thus, at the time you purchase a pass-through certificate it is impossible to know the price you will receive in the event you are required to sell it prior to a full payoff. If you hold a certificate for any length of time, you will almost certainly receive less than you paid, because a portion of the principal amount of the underlying mortgages will already have been repaid.

Summary: Pass-through Certificates Pass-through certificates are high-quality securities that produce high yields and large monthly cash payments. The high yields are offset, at least in part, by uncertainty regarding the amount of cash that will be received in any particular month. Falling market rates of interest tend to produce rapid repayment at a time when you least desire it. The likelihood of prepayments can be minimized by choosing participation certificates in pools comprised of low-interest mortgages.

Long-Term Bonds

Chapter 3 describes the features, yields, and risks of intermediate-term debt securities issued by corporations, municipal governments, federal agencies, and the U.S. Treasury. These same organizations also issue bonds, debt securities with maturities longer than ten years. These long-term securities have the same basic characteristics as notes, only exaggerated. Long-term bonds are subject to bigger price fluctuations, a disadvantage if you may need to sell a bond prior to maturity. The longer the maturity length, the larger the price fluctuations. Many long-term corporate and municipal bonds are traded infrequently and these may have to be sold at a reduced price. Long-term bonds also suffer a greater degree of purchasing-power risk because fixed payments occur over such a long period. How much will the $5,000 principal of a municipal bond be worth at maturity in twenty-five years? Although the credit risk (that is, the risk of not getting paid) varies with a bond's issuer, long-term bonds tend to entail more credit risk than intermediate-term bonds of the same issuers. Many unexpected events can occur in twenty-five years.

On the positive side, a bondholder stands to earn a higher return than the owner of a note. Longer maturities are nearly always accompanied by higher current yields. Large price fluctuations may allow you to supplement interest income with increases in the market value of the securities if market interest rates decline. Changes in value are not particularly important if you plan to hold the bonds to maturity, although a price decline may cause you to feel poorer.

Most long-term corporate debt is issued with a call feature that permits the issuer to retire the securities at a predetermined price before maturity. A call feature is nearly always to your disadvantage, because a call is most likely to occur after interest rates have declined and the issuer can borrow at a reduced interest rate. Being forced to sell the bond back to the issuer means you must reinvest the proceeds at a return lower than that provided by the called bond. Many corporate notes and some bonds are issued without a call feature, meaning that you will be able to hold these securities to the scheduled maturity.

CHAPTER 5

Investment Companies and Trusts That Provide Current Income

Investment companies and trusts are popular alternatives to direct ownership of stocks, bonds, and other financial assets. Interest and dividend income and realized gains from financial assets owned by the investment companies are periodically paid out to the owners. Investment companies and trusts offer professional asset selection and diversification that most investors could not otherwise obtain. Many have specialized portfolios that contain particular categories of investments including those that provide high current yields that were discussed in the previous chapters. Investment companies and unit trusts are attractive choices for individuals who lack the knowledge or time to choose their own investments.

Some businesses invest in land, buildings, and machines in order to manufacture and sell products. Investment companies (as discussed in this chapter) put their capital into financial assets such as common stocks, preferred stocks, notes and bonds. Instead of mining copper, manufacturing automobiles, or selling groceries, investment companies and investment trusts use money from individual investors such as you to assemble portfolios of financial assets.

Investment companies and investment trusts are available to meet nearly any investment need. Investment companies specialize in growth stocks, utility stocks, health company stocks, junk (low-quality) bonds, or in investments in Korea, the Pacific Basin, Europe, Australia, or New York. Investment trusts specialize in corporate bonds, junk bonds, U.S. Treasury bonds, municipal bonds, and real estate debt. Investment company shares and trust units are sold by insurance companies, financial planners, brokerage companies, and by mail. Thousands of these companies have been formed to invest your money and allow you to share in the profits and losses from their investments. Investment companies and trusts don't just provide advice on how to invest your money, they invest for you!

Many investment companies and trusts specialize in investments that provide high current yields. You can choose an investment company or unit investment trust that invests in long-term corporate bonds, intermediate-term corporate notes and bonds, Treasury securities, municipal bonds, or municipal notes. Rather than a $10,000 investment in the notes or bonds of a single company or a single city or county, investment company shares and trust units provide you with part ownership in portfolios that are likely to include hundreds of different income stocks, preferred stocks, or bond issues. You can choose to invest in an investment company that continually monitors and manages the securities in its portfolio or you can choose an investment trust that assembles a portfolio that remains unchanged until the bonds mature and your principal is returned. Investment companies and trusts also provide an opportunity to earn high levels of current income by owning shares in diversified portfolios of long-term investments, intermediate-term investments, and short-term investments.

The value of your investment in an investment company or investment trust is affected by changes in the market value of the portfolio that is held. If you have invested in an investment company that holds a portfolio of long-term bonds and market rates of interest increase, the value of your investment will decline. If the firm holds a portfolio of intermediate-term bonds the same increase in interest rates would produce a smaller decline in the value of the portfolio and the value of your investment. The bottom line is, your investment in an investment company or an investment trust is tied to the fortunes of the portfolio of which you are part owner.

Fundamentals of Investment Companies

An investment company holds a portfolio of financial assets that is actively managed by professional investment man-

Corporate and government notes with maturities of three to eight years are often a good compromise between the low yields and stable values of short-term investments and the high yields and unstable values of many long-term investments.

agers for the benefit of the company's owners. Financial assets are acquired using money contributed by investors who purchase shares in an investment company. Shares of ownership entitle the investors to proportional distributions of interest, dividend income, or both, and to realized gains from the sale of assets.

Many investment companies levy a sales charge or a redemption fee. All investment company sponsors levy an annual charge to cover operating and management costs and earn a profit for the sponsors. Someone has to pay for the paperwork, postage, salaries, phone calls, rent, and so forth. Annual charges generally range from one-fourth of 1 percent to more than 1 percent of a fund's assets. The bigger the fund, the more money for the sponsor. An annual fee charged against the company's income is a direct reduction in the yield you will earn from owning the company's shares. If an investment company holds a bond portfolio with a 7 percent yield, an annual charge of three-fourths of 1 percent will reduce the yield earned by the company's shareholders to 6¼ percent.

Federal regulations require that investment companies pay current income and realized gains (gains and losses are only realized when investments are sold) to their shareholders who bear the tax consequences. For example, an investment company that holds bonds in its portfolio must

---

If you have difficulty comparing the quoted yields on certificates of deposit at different institutions, ask how much money will be in your account at the end of one year, two years, or however long your money will be on deposit. The bottom line is the amount of money you will have available when the certificate matures.

distribute to the owners interest income that is collected from the bonds. The higher the yields that are earned from the bonds in the portfolio, the more interest that is passed through to the owners. Likewise, an investment company with a portfolio of income stocks or preferred stocks distributes to its shareholders the dividend income that is collected. Investment companies that hold portfolios of high-yielding bonds and stocks make relatively high current-income payments to their shareholders.

Investment companies also distribute to owners the realized gains from securities that are sold. These gains are taxable to the investors who receive them, not the investment company that distributes them. Gains in the value of assets that remain in a portfolio (sometimes called *paper gains*) increase the value of the company's portfolio and the value of its shares of ownership, but do not result in a distribution or a tax consequence to shareholders.

Two Types of Investment Companies

Two types of investment companies sell shares to the public; mutual funds and closed-end investment companies. Both organizations have certain common characteristics, but at the same time, important differences exist, especially with regard to how their shares are valued and redeemed. Both varieties of investment companies attempt to select and manage their portfolios in such a manner that shareholder value is enhanced.

Mutual Funds Mutual funds (also called *open-end investment companies*) are organized with a flexible number of ownership shares. This type of investment company continues to sell additional shares to either existing or new investors while it stands ready to redeem outstanding shares. An investment in a mutual fund can be liquidated by selling shares back to the company. An initial offering of shares is sold to investors but subsequent sales and redemptions cause the size of a mutual fund's portfolio to expand and contract. A net inflow of funds that results when sales exceed redemptions is invested in additional securities, which are added to the existing portfolio. A net outflow of funds caused by a net redemption of investment company shares requires a fund to sell a portion of its investment portfolio to raise the money needed to pay the sellers. Neither a net inflow or net outflow affects the value of a mutual fund's shares because of proportional changes in both the value of the portfolio and the number of shares. A mutual fund can double the number of shares and double the size of its portfolio without affecting the value of each share.

Some mutual funds choose to distribute their shares through sales groups that receive a sales fee from an added charge, or *load,* that is paid by investors who purchase the shares. Sales fees of up to 8½ percent are sometimes charged although sales charges generally average 4 percent or less for funds that specialize in bond investments. Other funds sell shares directly to investors and may or may not charge a sales fee. Mutual funds that do not charge a sales fee are called *no-load funds* and those with relatively low sales fees are called *low-load funds*. Sales fees increase the amount of money you must pay to purchase a given number of shares or reduce the number of shares you can purchase with a given amount of money.

Mutual fund shares are sold at *net asset value* (NAV) plus any sales fee. Shares are also redeemed at net asset value, although some funds levy a redemption fee. Net asset value is the market value of the fund's portfolio divided by the outstanding number of the fund's shares. If a mutual fund with 10 million shares outstanding holds a bond portfolio with a market value of $200 million, the net asset value is $200 million divided by 10 million, or $20. If the fund levies a 3 percent load, only $9,700 of your $10,000 investment will go to purchase shares in the fund.

Closed-End Investment Companies Closed-end investment companies sell a fixed number of shares which are subsequently traded in the secondary market. Shares of these firms can be purchased only from the investment banker who underwrites a new issue or in the secondary market from other investors. Shares cannot be purchased directly from the company following the original issue and cannot be sold back to the company when you decide to liquidate your investment. Closed-end investment companies do not redeem their own shares, so you must use the services of a brokerage company to locate another investor willing to buy your shares. Shares in the secondary market often sell at prices above or below their net asset value, depending on investment demand. Closed-end investment companies charge their shareholders an annual management fee and investors must pay a brokerage fee to buy or sell the shares.

The price at which the shares of a closed-end investment company trade in the secondary market is a function of sev-

Most long-term bonds are subject to being redeemed early by the issuer. A call can result in a loss of the principal amount of your investment if you have paid above face value for a bond. Always inquire about the call provision before you invest in a bond, especially if the bond sells at a premium.

eral factors, including the market value of its portfolio, income produced by the portfolio, and the perceived quality of the firm's management. Investors may not be willing to pay full price (net asset value) for a closed-end investment company that has produced poor investment results over an extended period. Why buy into a portfolio that is poorly managed? On the other hand, investors are likely to be willing to pay a premium for the shares of a well-managed closed-end investment company.

Figure 24 illustrates published price quotations for a variety of closed-end investment companies, including investment grade bond funds, high-yield bond funds, national municipal bond funds, and single-state municipal bond funds. These quotations are published by the *Wall Street Journal* and some major metropolitan newspapers, generally weekly. Share prices and trading volume are published in daily stock listings. Each listing in Figure 24 includes the name of the investment company, the exchange on which the company's stock is traded, and net asset value per share (that is, total assets divided by shares outstanding), the market price at which the shares trade, and the premium or discount of the market price compared to the net asset value. For example, the first listing, for Ft Dearborn, indicates a stock with a net asset value of $15.06 per share and a market price of $14.00 per share. The shares are trading at a 7 percent discount from net asset value.

Make it a regular habit to read one or two periodicals dealing with personal investing. It is also a good idea to acquire several books that provide general information on personal investing. Skip books and articles that promote get-rich-quick schemes.

Figure 24

PUBLISHED PRICE QUOTATIONS FOR
CLOSED-END INVESTMENT COMPANIES
(Partial Listing for Companies with Various Goals)

Fund Name	Stock Exchange	NAV	Market Price	Premium/ Discount
Ft Dearborn Inc	NYSE	15.06	14	- 7.0
Montgomery St	NYSE	18.49	16⅝	-10.1
Corp Hi Yld	NYSE	12.87	11½	-10.6
Kemper Strat Inc	NYSE	13.55	11¾	+ 1.5
USLife Income	NYSE	9.32	8⅜	-10.1
MFS Muni Inco	NYSE	8.84	9⅜	+ 6.1
Dreyfus NY Inc	ASE	9.92	9⅛	- 8.0
Nuveen CA Inc	NYSE	11.72	11⅝	- 0.8
Ellsworth Conv	ASE	9.73	8⅝	-11.4

Real estate investment trusts (REITs) are a specialized type of closed-end investment company. *Equity trusts* own property and collect rents that are distributed to the REIT owners. *Mortgage trusts* make mortgage loans and collect interest income that is then paid out to the REIT owners. Both types of investment companies can be risky with respect to income and principal, depending on the particular properties or mortgages the trusts own. Vacancies in owned properties or nonpayment by borrowers will negatively affect distributions to REIT owners. Some trusts utilize substantial amounts of debt, further increasing the risk of owning one of these investments. On the positive side, REITs can produce hefty cash flows and equity trusts can experience substantial price appreciation. REIT shares are relatively liquid. Some are listed on the New York Stock Exchange, while others are traded on the American Stock Exchange and the over-the-counter market. Unfortunately, real estate investment trusts can be very risky and you should generally avoid these investments unless you thoroughly understand what you are buying. The riskiness of the investment is greatly affected by the type of REIT (equity or mortgage) and the degree to which leverage is used to finance the REIT.

Unit Investment Trusts Unit investment trusts (also called *unit trusts* or *investment trusts*) are unmanaged investment portfolios. Unit investment trusts have an organizational structure that is different from that of investment companies, but unit trusts have been included in this section because they are direct competitors with both mutual funds and closed-end investment companies, especially those specializing in fixed-income investments. The sponsor of a unit trust assembles a portfolio of assets (municipal bonds, corporate bonds, U.S. Treasury securities, and so forth) and sells a fixed number of ownership units (they actually are called *units*) to individual investors. All income and principal received by the trust are paid to investors who own the units. When a bond held by a trust is redeemed by the is-

Buying bonds in the primary market will save you a brokerage commission and is likely to provide a slightly higher yield than you can earn from bonds being offered in the secondary market. Ask a broker about upcoming bond issues when you are interested in a fixed-income investment.

Figure 25

PROFILES OF INVESTMENT COMPANIES AND TRUSTS

Mutual Fund
- Redeems shares at net asset value
- May require a sales fee to purchase or a redemption fee
- May charge an annual 12b-1 marketing fee
- Continually issues additional shares
- Actively manages investment portfolio

Closed-End Investment Company
- Number of shares outstanding is limited
- Shares are traded in the secondary market
- Shares may trade at a price other than net asset value
- Purchase or sale of shares requires a brokerage commission
- Investment portfolio is actively managed

Investment Trust
- Investment portfolio is unmanaged
- Charges no annual management fee
- Requires a sales fee to purchase
- Distributes both interest and principal
- Makes a good choice for a long holding period
- Sponsor generally maintains a secondary market

---

suer, either at maturity or through a call, money collected from the redemption is distributed on a proportional basis to investors holding units of the trust. As principal is repaid, the portfolio gradually dissolves over the years and unit values decline. Passing through principal repayments contrasts with investment companies that reinvest the principal in additional securities. Investment companies are ongoing entities while trusts are scheduled to vanish eventually.

Unit trusts are particularly popular among investors who seek current interest income from bonds because of the relatively small investment that is required to acquire partial ownership in a diversified bond portfolio. Units usually sell for approximately $1,000. The relative advantage of the small required investment is particularly appealing for investors who seek tax-exempt interest income, because municipal bonds must normally be purchased in much larger denominations. Unit trust sponsors charge a sales fee of approximately 4 percent of the amount invested although no management fees or redemption fees are levied (there is no ongoing portfolio management). Units can generally be resold through the sponsor, who usually maintains a secondary market.

Unit values vary with the aggregate value of the underlying portfolio held by the trust. Falling interest rates increase the value of a trust's bond portfolio, which, in turn, causes an increase in the value of the trust's outstanding units. Financial difficulty of a municipal government or corporation that has issued bonds held in a trust's portfolio is likely to cause a decline in the value of the trust's units. Buying units of a trust is nothing other than purchasing a small proportional ownership in an existing portfolio of investments. Anything that affects the value of the portfolio affects the value of the units you own.

Unit investment trusts are generally preferred to mutual funds and closed-end investment companies when you are investing for current income and plan a long holding period. Unit trusts have no annual management fee to eat away at the return you earn.

Choosing Investment Companies for Current Income

Regardless of the type of current-income investment you are thinking about buying, an investment company or trust with a ready-made portfolio of that same investment is almost certainly available. Investment companies specialize in tax-exempt municipal bonds, corporate bonds, income stocks, and preferred stocks. Among investment companies that specialize in municipal bonds, some companies specialize in the bonds of a particular state (so you will earn interest income that is exempt from both federal and state taxes), bonds of a particular maturity length, bonds of a particular credit quality, and so forth. Investment companies specialize in junk bonds, investment-grade bonds, long-term bonds, intermediate-term bonds, and on and on. Unit trusts are also offered in specialized form. There seems to be no end to which sponsors of investment companies and trusts will go to attract investors who seek specialized investments. No matter what type of current-income investment you desire, an investment company that specializes in the same type of investment is almost certainly available.

Diversification

Ready-made portfolios offer investors who seek current investment income several advantages over individual securities. Probably most important is the reduced risk involved in owning securities from a large number of different issuers. Owning securities from many different issuers reduces the possibility that financial difficulty of one or two particular issuers will produce a major loss in your investment holdings. Having 50 percent of your portfolio in each of two investments offers the potential for much greater losses (and profits) than having an ownership interest in a portfolio of a hundred or more different investments. Financial experts advise that at least eight to ten different bond issues are required to produce a properly diversified portfolio. With municipal bonds selling in $5,000 denominations, you would have to commit at least $40,000 (8 times $5,000) to own the recommended number of different bonds.

On the other hand, you can invest a relatively small amount in an investment company and have part interest in a diversified portfolio that may contain dozens or even hundreds of different bond issues. Different investment companies have different investment requirements, both to open an account and to add to an account. It is not unusual to be able to open a mutual fund account with an initial investment of $1,000 (some require only $250, while others require $2,500 and up) and to make subsequent investments of much smaller amounts. Any number of shares in a closed-end investment company can be purchased, although small purchases result in relatively high brokerage commissions. Trust units normally sell for $1,000, but you initially may have to purchase more than a single unit. Still, each of these choices allows you to gain the advantage of diversification with a relatively small investment.

If in doubt about where to put your money, choose a familiar investment that you are comfortable owning. Better to lose a little current income and sleep well than to be in a state of perpetual worry about the safety of your investments.

Professional Selection and Management

Investment companies and investment trusts both offer professionally selected portfolios. Professionals choose the bonds, stocks, or other investments that make up a particular investment. Direct investing requires you to choose the investments for your own portfolio. Of course, you can rely on the advice of your broker or a friend, but you are likely to find it difficult to construct an efficient portfolio. Most individual investors have difficulty constructing a portfolio of investments that really fit together. Investment company managers not only construct the initial portfolio but also oversee and manage the investments on an ongoing basis. Someone who makes a living working in the financial markets should be one of the first to discover trends and news affecting particular companies or industries.

Expenses

Diversification and professional portfolio management come at a price. Choosing to place your funds with an investment company or a unit trust entails expenses you could avoid by investing directly. The fees you may be required to pay to purchase investment company shares or trust units cause you to pay a greater amount for a given portfolio value than would be required for a direct investment. Likewise, annual fees to manage an investment company cause a direct reduction in the yield you earn. An investment company with a bond portfolio that earns an 8 percent return from interest income will retain a portion of the income to cover its expenses. You may end up with a return of 7 percent or 7½ percent from interest income that is distributed to shareholders after expenses. The effective return will be reduced even more if you pay a 12b-1 fee to cover distribution expenses.

Expenses have the potential to consume a significant portion of the return you earn, so you should carefully investigate all of the potential charges for investing before parting with your money. Different investment companies have virtually identical portfolios but charge different expense ratios. Differing expenses are one of the primary reasons for differing yields among investment companies that hold bond portfolios. You are likely to earn a superior current yield from a unit trust as opposed to an investment company if you hold an investment for many years.

Locating Information about
Investment Companies and Trusts

Investment company share prices are published in many daily newspapers, including the *Wall Street Journal*. The tremendous growth in the number of mutual funds makes it impossible for publications to publish a complete listing, but the most popular companies are generally included. Mutual fund prices are published in a section devoted exclusively to these investments. The listing for each fund generally includes the previous day's net asset value (NAV) and, less frequently, the change from the prior day's net asset value.

Share prices for closed-end investment companies are published in the listings of stocks traded on the organized exchanges. Published information is identical to that for the shares of General Motors, AT&T, or any other publicly traded stock. Market values for units of investment trusts generally must be obtained from the sponsor of the trust.

Determining which one or two of the thousands of available investment companies or trusts best meets your needs is a daunting task even for a professional investor. Nearly five thousand mutual funds alone are currently available for purchase. Additional alternatives among closed-end funds and unit trusts make the decision process even more formidable.

Several financial information services provide data and recommendations regarding mutual funds, the most popular ready-made portfolios. The best-known services devoted exclusively to mutual funds are *The Value Line Mutual Fund Survey*, the *Morningstar Mutual Funds,* and *Investment Companies* by Arthur Wisenberger Services. These services are all excellent and include most of the information you will need to make an investment decision. Many public and college libraries subscribe to one or more of the services, which frequently offer low-cost trial subscriptions. Information and data on mutual funds, including sales fees, management expenses, and short- and long-term performance are published periodically by *Forbes, Business Week, Money,* and *Kiplinger's Personal Finance Magazine*. Many investment newsletters of varying quality and usefulness cater to the needs of mutual fund investors.

Beware of a broker or an investment adviser who attempts to steer you to investments you would generally avoid or don't understand. A broker's income is determined by commissions earned from investments the broker sells. Certain investment products involve high commissions that benefit the broker more than the customer.

The Guide to Investing for Current Income

Making an Investment Decision

With the large number of investment companies available and the countless sources of investment advice how should you go about making a choice? Here are some points to consider:

1. Narrow your choices to investment companies and investment trusts with investment goals that are compatible with your needs. Assuming you are interested in current income, investment companies that invest in growth funds can be ruled out, for example. Likewise, if earning tax-free income is important, chose among investment companies and trusts that invest in municipal bonds. If fluctuations in value cause you worry, stay away from investment companies and investment trusts that hold portfolios of long-term bonds or stocks.

2. Further narrow your alternatives to investment companies and trusts that invest in securities you consider suitable for the risks you can safely assume. A need for secure income and reasonable stability of principal should warn you to avoid investment companies that own junk bond portfolios. A desire for ultrasafety of income and principal might lead you to an investment company or trust that invests in U.S. Treasury notes with relatively short maturities.

The current yield is often a misleading measure of the total yield you will earn from owning a particular investment. A bond selling above par may offer a very high current yield but a relatively low total yield. Ask about an investment's total yield (in the case of a bond, the yield to maturity or yield to call) as well as the current yield.

3. Review the investment performance of an investment company over a period of many years, not just the last year or two. Short-term investment results are generally considered a poor indicator for forecasting an investment company's future performance. For example, don't choose a particular investment company because of last year's above-average investment performance. Also, make certain you are comparing apples with apples, not apples with oranges. That is, compare the performance of long-term bond funds with other long-term bond funds, not with intermediate-term bond funds. Likewise, judge the investment performance of a junk bond fund against other junk bond funds, not against investment companies with portfolios of high-grade corporate bonds or Treasury securities.

4. Pay particular attention to the fees an investment company charges. Sales fees, redemption fees, operating fees, and 12b-1 distribution fees all reduce the return you will earn on your investment. Investment companies operate in a very competitive environment and some fund sponsors attempt to attract investors by keeping expenses to a minimum. Low expenses are particularly important among investment companies with the investment goal to produce current income. Search diligently and you will find excellent companies with no sales or redemption fees and modest operating fees.

5. Search for investment companies that are members of a family of funds—a group of investment companies with a variety of investment goals offered by the same sponsor. Sponsors will often allow you to transfer your investment among different investment companies operated by the same sponsor at low cost. Thus, you can accumulate shares of an investment company with a portfolio of intermediate-

term bonds and later transfer a portion of your investment to an investment company with a portfolio of long-term bonds. It is convenient to transfer funds from one investment company to another by telephone without incurring an additional sales charge.

CHAPTER 6

Constructing a Current-Income Investment Portfolio

Intelligent investment selection can reduce the risks associated with owning a portfolio that produces current income. A portfolio of high-quality fixed-income investments with staggered maturities provides a combination of security, liquidity, and yield. Alternating interest payment dates or dividend payment dates can produce a steady monthly income. An emergency fund of current-income investments with high liquidity should be maintained at all times, even though the yield is likely to be relatively low.

Even though you have decided to concentrate on purchasing current income investments, other important decisions remain to be made. You must choose which among the numerous investment alternatives discussed in previous chapters best meet your investment needs. What level of credit risk do you find acceptable, for example? The more risk you are willing to accept, the higher the return you can expect. If you choose to purchase bonds, should you go with the higher yields available on longer maturities, or should you play it safe and select bonds with intermediate-length maturities? Is the credit quality of Treasury securities worth the lower yield available on these securities? Will you come out ahead by investing in tax-exempt municipal securities or should you stick with higher-yielding corporate bonds? Is the diversification afforded by mutual funds worth the management fee you will be charged? If you choose the mutual fund route, which fund should you purchase? Or would you be better off choosing an investment trust or closed-end investment company?

There is no way to know *exactly* which current income investment to choose, of course, but some general guidelines can be used to develop an overall portfolio strategy.

- Realize that fixed income doesn't mean fixed purchasing power. Long-term fixed cash streams gradually lose value as inflation eats away at purchasing power. Betting the farm on long-term fixed-income investments is very risky and generally unwise.

Don't be greedy! Greed has been the downfall for many individual investors who wanted to become as rich as possible as rapidly as possible.

Constructing a Current-Income Investment Portfolio

- Don't invest in intermediate- and long-term securities or mutual funds that own these securities until you have an adequate emergency fund of liquid investments. You don't want to be placed in the position of being required to sell long-term investments in order to meet short-term needs.
- Choose new investments on the basis of investments you already hold. Portfolio building, whether for current income, capital growth, or tax savings, is an ongoing task and additions should improve the overall portfolio. The choice of a new asset should take into account assets you already own.
- Don't sacrifice yield for added liquidity if your investment portfolio already has substantial liquidity. Adding liquidity on top of liquidity causes a reduction in return without an offsetting gain in risk reduction. Investing a substantial proportion of a large portfolio in a money market fund or short-term CDs doesn't ordinarily make sense.
- Generally avoid unrated current-income securities. Quality grades provided by credit-rating agencies provide an unbiased guide to a security's credit quality. Some unrated securities are perfectly safe, but owning them involves potential pitfalls that only experts can identify. Stay away.
- Don't reach for high yields at the expense of safety. It is tempting to lower your own credit standards in order to gain a higher yield, especially when interest rates are declining and you are accustomed to earning higher returns. This is a mistake. Determine the appropriate credit risk and stick with it.
- Realize that even the "safest" current-income investments can experience substantial fluctuations in value if maturities are long. Long-term U.S. Treasury securities

have no credit risk but move up and down in price as market rates of interest change.

- Acquire notes, bonds, and certificates of deposit with the idea that you will hold them to maturity. Commissions and penalties are nearly always incurred when it is necessary to sell bonds and redeem CDs before their scheduled maturities. Choose maturities so you will not have to redeem securities in order to meet short-term needs.

- Don't acquire tax-exempt investments unless the benefits of the tax savings more than offset the lower yields. Tax-exemption is best left to individual investors with substantial amounts of taxable income.

- Keep the shape of the yield curve in mind when you are selecting maturity lengths. Yields often rise rapidly as you extend maturity lengths up to ten or twelve years. Yields generally rise more gradually as you extend maturities beyond twelve years. This "kink" is found at different points in the curve but generally occurs at maturities between eight and twelve years. You can obtain the best combination of yield and maturity length by purchasing investments with maturities near the kink.

- Build a portfolio of "laddered" maturities: A portfolio that includes short-term, intermediate-term, and long-term investments provides a good combination of yield,

Evaluate the returns from current-income investments on an after-tax basis. Taxes can eat away a substantial proportion of the income you earn. Tax-exempt investments can provide a higher after-tax income than taxable investments, especially if you are in a high tax bracket.

stability of value, and liquidity. Laddering is discussed in more detail below.

- Choose investment companies or investment trusts if you will be investing relatively modest amounts of money. Individual issues of bonds and notes involve relatively large amounts of money that make it difficult to achieve adequate diversification. Focus on minimizing sales charges and management fees when choosing these investments.

Building a Laddered Portfolio

The trade-off between yield and liquidity has been discussed several times. Investments with longer maturities generally provide higher current yields but often lack the liquidity of short-term investments. In addition, long-term assets are subject to substantial price fluctuations. Short-term investments have stable values and are easy to liquidate, but they earn relatively low returns that are seldom much above the inflation rate. Thus, selecting a current income investment forces you to choose between the price stability and liquidity of short-term assets and the relatively high current yields generally available on long-term assets. Can you have both? Perhaps, some of both.

Try to avoid mutual funds that charge annual 12b-1 distribution fees. These fees reduce the yield you will earn without providing any offsetting benefits. A fund's prospectus will tell you if a 12b-1 fee is charged and, if so, its size. These fees are calculated as a percentage of a fund's assets.

Building a laddered portfolio to provide current income from a series of securities that have successive maturities—a combination of short-, intermediate-, and long-term investments—is a good method for providing a balance between liquidity and yield. Long-term fixed-income assets provide high yields and short-term assets provide substantial liquidity. Intermediate-term assets provide a little of each. Maturity lengths of each of the securities in your portfolio gradually shorten over time, causing them to exhibit increasing price stability while the current yield based on the original purchase price remains unchanged. A bond that has a maturity of fifteen years and a coupon of 8 percent at the time of purchase eventually has a maturity of ten years, and, later, five years, but the 8 percent coupon and $80 annual interest payment remain the same.

Suppose you have accumulated $200,000 that is invested in six-month certificates of deposit that are currently providing a 4 percent annual return. You would like to earn a higher level of income but you don't want to surrender the safety of income and principal of the insured CDs, and you want to maintain a reasonable degree of liquidity. A potential solution is to place $20,000 in a money market fund or money market deposit account to provide for liquidity and stability of value, and invest the remaining $180,000 in $20,000 increments of Treasury securities maturing every other year. You would purchase $20,000 of Treasuries ma-

Stay up-to-date on market rates of interest. A knowledge of the yields that are available is important when selecting the best investment.

Figure 26

LADDERED PORTFOLIO OF
U.S. TREASURY SECURITIES

Maturity	Coupon	Face Amount	Price	Investment	Income
Oct 96	6⅞	$ 20,000	100:22	$ 20,138	$ 1,375
Oct 98	7⅛	20,000	100:12	20,075	1,425
Nov 00	8½	20,000	105:29	20,181	1,700
Aug 02	6⅜	20,000	93:16	18,700	1,275
Aug 04	7¼	20,000	97:30	19,587	1,450
Nov 06 *	14	15,000	148:18	22,205	2,100
Aug 08 *	13	15,000	134:13	20,161	1,950
Nov 09 *	11¾	15,000	133:31	20,095	1,762
May 16	7¼	20,000	92:29	18,581	1,450
Bond Total		$165,000		$179,723	$14,487
Money Market Fund @ 4½ percent				20,277	912
Investment Total				$200,000	$15,399

Current Yield = $15,399/$200,000 = 7.7 percent

* The maturity length is longer than indicated but the bond is callable on this date.

turing in two years, $20,000 of Treasuries maturing in four years, $20,000 of Treasuries maturing in six years, and so forth. With very-short-term securities as part of the portfolio, you may not need to maintain such a large money market account. Reducing the money market investment would allow you to improve your current yield by placing additional funds in long-term bonds. Figure 26 illustrates a laddered portfolio of Treasury securities.

The laddered portfolio of Figure 26 was constructed in the fall of 1994. The portfolio requires a $179,723 initial investment in U.S. Treasury securities and slightly over $20,000 in a money market fund. Annual interest income of $15,399 represents a current yield of 7.7 percent on the $200,000 investment, substantially higher than the 4 percent being earned on short-term certificates of deposit. Note that several bonds have a purchase price above par (these bonds were issued when interest rates were high), which means you would receive less money from redemption at maturity than you invested. The yield to maturity on a premium bond is less than the current yield. Also note that bonds with the longest maturities are not spaced exactly two years apart because of a lack of availability of Treasury bonds with the exact maturities required. High-grade corporate bonds with maturity dates in the years 2010 and 2012 could be substituted for the Treasury issues maturing in 2009 and 2016.

In October of 1996, when bonds with the shortest maturities are redeemed by the Treasury at maturity, the $20,000 of principal that is received can be spent or reinvested in additional Treasury bonds with a maturity approximately two years longer than the longest maturity remaining in the portfolio. In other words, you roll the principal forward into another Treasury security with a long maturity. Adding

Investment companies that are just starting up will sometimes attempt to attract investors by waiving their management fees for the first year or so. Waivers of this fee will temporarily result in a higher return than you would otherwise earn. When the fee is imposed (usually gradually), you may want to transfer your funds to a different investment company.

long-term bonds allows you to continue to earn a high current yield. The bond that had a four-year maturity length at the time you established the portfolio will now have a two-year maturity length (two years have passed since the portfolio was constructed).

A laddered portfolio helps protect your current income from a decline in market interest rates. If rates fall and you are required to reinvest redeemed bonds in new bonds that have reduced yields, you still have interest income provided by bonds that were purchased at the earlier date. You don't have to worry about being required to reinvest all of your funds at the same time—a nightmare if interest rates have experienced a major decline. At the same time, you don't have to be concerned with rising interest rates that deplete the market values of your bonds. You won't have to sell the bonds in a depressed market because some of your bonds will be continually redeemed.

Other fixed-income securities can be substituted for the Treasuries used in Figure 26. For example, you can use preferred stocks or income stocks to substitute for bonds at the long end of the maturity ladder. Likewise, you could construct a laddered portfolio of high-grade corporate bonds or municipal bonds. Corporate bonds would provide a higher current yield than Treasuries (although Treasury interest is

---

The greater your reliance on investment income and the more damaging a loss of principal would be, the more you should strive for safety at the expense of higher yields. A percentage point or two in extra return isn't worth a greater likelihood that you will suffer an income reduction (a dividend reduction, say) or a loss of principal.

free of state and local taxes) and municipal bonds would pay interest income that is exempt from federal income taxes and perhaps state taxes. The choice of securities should be a function of your willingness to assume credit risk and of your state and federal tax situation. When investment income is required to meet living expenses, it is wise to choose high-quality investments for the portfolio.

If liquidity is important and only a nominal amount of money is available for investing, begin building the laddered portfolio from the near term out. That is, first accumulate an appropriate amount in a money market fund or money market deposit account for emergency purposes, then purchase two-year bonds, followed by four-year bonds, and so forth. Build the portfolio outward, not inward. It is risky to make your first purchase twenty-year bonds that have a high current yield but are subject to major fluctuations in value. Alternatively, with only nominal investment capital available it is probably best to use investment companies to build a current-income portfolio.

Building a Current-Income Portfolio with Investment Companies

Investment companies provide a more flexible method for building a laddered portfolio of current-income investments. Rather than investing in ten to twelve different individual is-

A portfolio of substantial size can be arranged to provide relatively equal monthly income payments by selecting bonds or stocks with appropriate payment dates.

sues of fixed-income securities with varying maturities, you can concentrate your investments in a money market fund, an intermediate-term fund or trust, and a long-term fund or trust. For example, the initial $200,000 investment discussed above could be allocated 10 percent to a money market fund, 40 percent to an intermediate-term bond fund or unit trust, and 50 percent to a long-term bond fund or unit trust. Allocation among the funds can be easily altered as your spending needs and investment goals change.

An investment company continually adjusts its portfolio to achieve the stated investment goal. Thus, the manager of a long-term bond fund sells bonds with maturities that have become too short and uses funds received from redemptions to acquire additional bonds with long maturities. This doesn't mean the average maturity of a bond portfolio never changes, it does. It does mean that the portfolio of a long-term or intermediate-term bond fund isn't permitted to shorten to the point that a large portion of the bonds are near maturity. A long-term bond fund remains a long-term bond fund, even over a period of many years. The fund provides a current yield that is commensurate with the yields on individual bonds with long maturities. Likewise, the price of the fund's shares will fluctuate to the same extent that the market value of long-term bonds fluctuates.

Using investment companies and trusts significantly simplifies the task of building a current income investment portfolio. Once you have established an adequate emergency

> Change your broker if you aren't happy with the advice or assistance you are getting. Making a change will allow you to select someone who is more in tune with your investment goals.

fund, relatively small investments are required to establish a stake in long-term and intermediate-term investment companies and trusts. Equally important, you can add relatively small amounts to these investments whenever you like, not only when you have accumulated the extra $5,000 or $10,000 that would be required to purchase individual bond issues.

Investment companies and trusts that invest in bonds have different standards for the credit quality of the bonds they hold, so you must make certain that the quality of a portfolio matches your own need for credit quality. You should generally stick with investment companies and trusts that own mostly high-quality bonds, especially if current income you receive is required to meet regular spending needs. Remember that the flexibility, professional management, and diversification provided by investment companies and trusts comes at a price: fees that reduce the yield you receive. If you choose to use investment companies and trusts for building your current income portfolio, be certain to select firms that charge reasonable fees.

Brokerage firms often employ professional portfolio managers to construct current-income portfolios for investors who have substantial funds to invest. You will have to rely on the advice of your broker or on your own money smarts if you invest only modest amounts of money.

Glossary

above par Designation for a bond or preferred stock that sells at a price above face value.

baby bond A bond with a principal amount under $1,000.

balanced fund An investment company with a portfolio that includes both bonds and stocks.

basis The acquisition cost of an asset.

below par Designation for a bond or preferred stock that sells at a price below face value.

bond rating The credit quality of a bond as judged by one of the major credit-rating agencies. Also called *credit rating.*

bond swap Selling one bond and simultaneously buying another in order to benefit from different yields, different maturities, and so forth.

book-entry security A security for which no negotiable certificate is sent to the owner.

calendar A listing of upcoming bond issues.

call Early redemption of a bond or preferred stock.

call date The date on which debt or preferred stock may be redeemed by the issuer,

call premium The amount above face value that an issuer must pay to redeem a bond before maturity or to repurchase preferred stock.

capital gain The amount by which the current value of a capital asset exceeds the price that was paid for it.

capital loss The amount by which the current value of a capital asset is exceeded by the price paid for it.

closed-end investment company An investment firm that issues a limited number of ownership shares and whose shares are traded on an exchange or in the over-the-counter market.

collateralized mortgage obligation (CMO) A pass-through security classed according to expected maturity ranges. CMOs pay interest and principal in a more predictable manner than do the pass-through securities on which they are based.

commission The fee charged by a broker to execute a security trade.

convertible security A bond or preferred stock that can be exchanged for shares of the issuer's common stock.

corporate bond A debt security issued by a corporation. Also called a *corporate*.

coupon The annual interest paid on a debt security. The coupon is generally stated as a percentage of face value.

credit rating See *bond rating*.

cumulative Pertaining to preferred stock on which all dividends must be current before any dividends can be paid to common stockholders.

current yield The return on a bond calculated by dividing the annual interest by the bond's current market price.

debenture An unsecured bond.

denomination The face value of a bond.

discount bond A bond that sells below face value.

diversification The purchase of assets whose returns are not directly related in order to minimize risk.

dividend A portion of a company's profits that is paid to its shareholders. Companies typically pay quarterly dividends.

dividend payout ratio See *payout ratio*.

dividend yield The percentage yield from a share of common stock calculated as the annual dividend divided by the market price of the stock.

equivalent taxable yield The taxable return that is equivalent to a tax-exempt return.

ex-dividend Pertaining to shares of a stock or mutual fund that trade without the right to a specific dividend.

expense ratio An investment company's annual management fee and operating expenses expressed as a percentage of the firm's assets.

general obligation bond (GO) A municipal bond guaranteed by the full resources and taxing power of the issuer. Also called a *full-faith-and-credit bond.*

Ginnie Mae pass-through A security issued by the Government National Mortgage Association that is backed by VA (Veterns Administration) and FHA (Federal Housing Administration) mortgages. See also *pass-through security.*

income fund An investment company that selects investments that are expected to provide current income for the fund's shareholders.

income stock A common stock that pays a relatively high annual dividend in comparison to the stock price.

inflation An increase in the price level of goods and services.

interest rate risk The degree to which the market value of a fixed-income security is affected by changes in market rates of interest.

investment company A firm that pools investors' money in a professionally managed portfolio of securities.

investment-grade Description for a bond that is considered sufficiently creditworthy that it can be included in regulated institutional portfolios.

junk bond A bond of low credit quality.

liquidity The ease with which an investment can be bought and sold.

load fund A mutual fund that charges a sales fee.

low-load fund A mutual fund with a sales charge equal to 3 percent or less of the amount of money invested in shares of the fund.

long-term bond A debt security with a maturity of ten years or more.

management fee The charge assessed by managers of an investment company.

maturity date The date on which a bond is scheduled for redemption.

mortgage bond A bond secured by a lien on real assets.

municipal bond A bond issued by a state, city, or other nonfederal political entity.

municipal bond fund A mutual fund that owns a portfolio of municipal bonds.

mutual fund An investment company that continuously issues new shares and redeems outstanding shares.

net asset value (NAV) The market value of an investment company's assets divided by the number of shares that are outstanding.

no-load fund A mutual fund that does not levy a sales fee on shares that are sold.

noncallable bond A bond that cannot be redeemed by the issuer before maturity.

not rated Description for a bond that has not been graded for quality by one of the professional credit-rating agencies. Also called *unrated*.

over-the-counter market (OTC) A network of securities dealers connected by telephones and computers who buy and sell in selected securities.

par The face value of a bond or share of preferred stock.

pass-through security A type of investment that "passes through" payments from debtors so that the investors receive monthly interest and principal payments.

payment date The date on which a dividend is paid to stockholders.

payout ratio The proportion of income a firm pays in dividends. Also called the *dividend payout ratio*.

preferred stock A security indicating corporate ownership with priority to dividends and assets relative to common stock. Most preferred stock pays a fixed quarterly dividend.

premium bond A bond that sells for more than its face value.

prerefunded bond A bond secured by an escrow fund of U.S. government obligations that is sufficient to pay off the entire issue of refunded bonds at maturity.

primary market The market in which securities are initially issued to investors.

principal The face amount of a bond or certificate of deposit.

prospectus A document relating to a new securities issue that details the financial status, officers, and operations of the issuing firm.

proxy Written authority from a stockholder that permits someone else (usually a firm's management) to vote on corporate matters for the stockholder.

public offering The sale of investment securities to the general public.

purchasing-power risk The risk that payments from an investment will lose value because of unexpected inflation.

record date The date on which an investor must be listed as an owner of a company's securities in order to qualify for a dividend, annual report, or proxy.

redemption Retirement of a debt security.

revenue bond A municipal bond for which repayment of principal and interest depends on money that is generated by the particular project the bonds are used to finance.

risk Uncertainty regarding the return that will be earned from owning a particular investment.

secondary market The market in which outstanding securities are traded among investors and dealers.

Securities Investor Protection Corporation (SIPC) The government-sponsored organization that insures customer accounts at brokerage companies.

senior debt A class of debt that has priority over one or more other debt issues of the same borrower.

serial bonds Bonds of a single issue that are scheduled to mature sequentially.

subordinated debentures Unsecured debt instruments with a weak claim to payment.

term bonds An issue of bonds that all mature on the same date.

Treasury bill A short-term debt security of the U.S. Treasury that is issued at a discount from face value. Also called a *T-bill*.

Treasury bond A debt security of the U.S. Treasury that is issued with a maturity length of more than ten years.

Treasury note A debt security of the U.S. Treasury that is issued with a maturity of from two to ten years.

12b-1 fee A charge against assets by mutual funds to help pay for distribution expenses.

unit investment trust (UIT) An unmanaged portfolio of bonds selected by a sponsor who sells ownership units of the trust to the public.

unrated See *not rated*.

yield The percentage return on an investment. Several different methods can be used to calculate the yield on most investments.

yield curve A graphic representation of the relationship between the yield and maturity length of a particular type of debt security.

yield to maturity (YTM) A bond's annual return based on the current market price, the coupon, the face value, and the assumption that the bond will be held until maturity.

Index

About the Author

David L. Scott is Professor of Accounting and Finance at Valdosta State University, Valdosta, Georgia. He was born in Rushville, Indiana, and received degrees from Purdue University and Florida State University before earning a Ph.D. in economics from the University of Arkansas at Fayetteville.

Dr. Scott has written two dozen books on personal finance and investing, including seven earlier volumes in the Money Smarts series. He is also author of the best-seller *Wall Street Words* (Houghton Mifflin) and of *How Wall Street Works* (Probus Publishers). He regularly conducts workshops on topics related to personal finance.

Professor Scott and his wife, Kay, are the authors of the two-volume *Guide to the National Park Areas* published by the Globe Pequot Press. They spend their summers traveling throughout the United States and Canada in their fourth Volkswagen Camper.

Globe Pequot Business Books

If you have found *The Guide to Investing for Current Income* informative, please be sure to read the following Globe Pequot business books.

Money Smarts Series

The Guide to Personal Budgeting
How to Stretch Your Dollars Through Wise Money Management, $8.95
by David L. Scott

The Guide to Investing in Common Stocks
How to Build Your Wealth by Mastering the Basic Strategies, $8.95
by David L. Scott

The Guide to Investing in Bonds
How to Build Your Wealth by Mastering the Basic Strategies, $8.95
by David L. Scott

The Guide to Investing in Mutual Funds
How to Build Your Wealth by Mastering the Basic Strategies, $9.95
by David L. Scott

The Guide to Buying Insurance
How to Secure the Coverage You Need at An Affordable Price, $9.95
by David L. Scott

The Guide to Managing Credit
How to Stretch Your Dollars Through Wise Credit Management, $8.95
by David L. Scott

The Guide to Tax-Saving Investing
How to Build Your Wealth by Mastering the Basic Strategies, $9.95
by David L. Scott

For beginning investors we suggest
Learning to Invest
A Beginner's Guide to Building Personal Wealth, $9.95
by Beatson Wallace

To order any of these titles with MASTERCARD or VISA, call toll-free (800) 243–0495. Free shipping on three or more books ordered; $3.00 shipping charge per book on one or two books ordered. Connecticut residents add sales tax. Please request a complimentary catalogue of other quality Globe Pequot titles, which include books on travel, outdoor recreation, nature, gardening, cooking, nature, and more.

Prices and availability subject to change.